The Pigman & Me

Books by Paul Zindel

The Pigman
Outstanding Children's Books of 1968, *The New York Times*
Notable Children's Books, 1940–1970 (ALA)
Best of the Best for Young Adults, 1966–1988 (ALA)

My Darling, My Hamburger
Outstanding Children's Books of 1969, *The New York Times*

I Never Loved Your Mind
Outstanding Children's Books of 1970, *The New York Times*

The Effect of Gamma Rays on Man-in-the-Moon Marigolds
1971 Pulitzer Prize for Drama
Best American Play of 1970 (New York Drama Desk
Critics Circle Award)
Notable Books of 1971 (ALA)
Best of the Best for Young Adults 1966–1988 (ALA)

I Love My Mother
(a picture book, illustrated by John Melo)

Pardon Me, You're Stepping On My Eyeball!
Outstanding Children's Books of 1976, *The New York Times*
Best Books for Young Adults, 1976 (ALA)

Confessions of a Teenage Baboon
Best Books for Young Adults, 1977 (ALA)

The Undertaker's Gone Bananas

The Pigman's Legacy
Outstanding Children's Books of 1980, *The New York Times*
Best Books for Young Adults, 1980 (ALA)

A Star for the Latecomer
(with Bonnie Zindel)

The Girl Who Wanted a Boy

Harry and Hortense at Hormone High

To Take a Dare
(with Crescent Dragonwagon)
Best Books for Young Adults, 1982 (ALA)

The Amazing and Death-Defying Diary of Eugene Dingman
(A Charlotte Zolotow Book)
1988 Book for the Teen Age (New York Public Library)

A Begonia for Miss Applebaum
(A Charlotte Zolotow Book)
Best Books for Young Adults, 1989 (ALA)
1990 Book for the Teen Age (New York Public Library)

The Pigman & Me

PAUL ZINDEL

A Charlotte Zolotow Book
An Imprint of HarperCollins*Publishers*

Library of Congress Cataloging-in-Publication Data
Zindel, Paul.
    The pigman & me / Paul Zindel.
    p.   cm.
    "A Charlotte Zolotow book."
    Summary: An account of Paul Zindel's teenage years on Staten Island, when his life was
enriched by finding his own personal pigman, or mentor.
    ISBN 0-06-020857-0. — ISBN 0-06-020858-9 (lib. bdg.)
    1. Zindel, Paul—Biography—Youth—Juvenile literature.   2. Authors, American—20th
century—Biography—Juvenile literature.   3. Staten Island (New York, N.Y.)—Social life
and customs—Juvenile literature.   [1. Zindel, Paul—Childhood and youth.   2. Authors,
American.]   I. Title.   II. Title: Pigman and me.
PS3576.I518Z47   1992   91-35790
812'.54—dc20   CIP
[B]   AC

2   3   4   5   6   7   8   9   10
First American Edition, 1992

Attention any KIDS who may read this Book!!!

Eight hundred and fifty-three horrifying things had happened to me by the time I was a teenager. That was when I met my pigman, whose real name was Nonno Frankie. Of course, some of you don't even know what a pigman is, but I do, so it's my duty to warn you. Sooner or later one will come your way, and what you do when you meet him will be a matter of life or death. When your own personal pigman comes, you may not recognize him at first. He may appear when you're shooting spitballs in your history class, or taking too many free mints from the cashier's desk at your local hamburger hangout. Your parents may even invite your pigman into your home for tea and crumpets or a tour of their waxed-wood floors. If he shakes your hand you will feel a chill, but he'll warm you with his smile. He'll want you to be his friend, to follow him, and in his eyes you'll see angels and monsters. Your pigman will come to you when you need him most.

He'll make you cry but teach you the greatest secret of life.

If you haven't croaked before finishing this book, then you'll understand how I survived being a teenager, and you'll know this important secret. The Surgeon General has not found this book to be dangerous to your health, but that's probably because she hasn't gotten around to reading it yet.

Because this is an Autobiography I have to, really Tell the truth!

Sincerely,

Paul Zindel

CHAPTERS

CHAPTER ONE

The Bizarre Adventures of My Teenage Life Begin!

The morning I found my pet lizard, Albert, dead in my mother's coffee mug was the day I should've known I'd soon be meeting my pigman. The mug lay in the rear window of our beat-up Chevrolet, and it rolled this way and that as we rounded the curves of Victory Boulevard. Albert had been missing for weeks. We simply hit a pothole and his little body popped up out of the mug while my mother was singing, which is what she did a lot of whenever she wasn't threatening to commit suicide.

"Casey would waltz with the strawberry blonde," she sang, *"and the band played on. He'd glide 'cross the floor*

with the girl he adored, and the band played on. . . ."

Mom's short bobbed hair wiggled in the wind rushing through the open car windows. Her dark eyes scanned the roadway in front, afraid to miss a single speck of oncoming life. My sister, Betty, a year and a half older than me, sat upon one of our dumpy suitcases, staring forward. She was a very pretty and suspicious girl, with long Sheena-Queen-of-the-Jungle blond hair. Then there was me. Hair like a blond carrottop. A sensitive, slightly nice-looking boy, but I didn't know I was either at the time. Actually, I didn't think I cared very much how the world saw me then, but I realize now I *did* care very much. I mostly thought of myself as a tall, scraggly, ordinary teenager glimpsed in a funhouse mirror.

"Mom, could you stop someplace so I can bury Albert?"

"Of course, dear," my mother said.

She pulled the car over in front of a parked Good Humor truck. She and my sister licked Creamola bars while I laid Albert to rest in the soft, moist soil next to a wild daisy. I had bought the chameleon as a living souvenir during intermission at a performance of the Ringling Brothers and Barnum & Bailey Circus. Then I brought him home and housed him royally for four months in a luscious grass-and-twig–decorated pickle jar. I even fed him the most succulent flies and wasps I could catch, but he'd escaped at least once a month and hidden in the faded lace curtains of our last rented apartment. He was mind-bogglingly hard to find, which, I imagine is precisely what God had in mind when he designed chameleons.

After Albert's funeral, we got back into the car, which was filled with everything we owned. We had just been evicted because Mother called the landlady a "snooping, vicious, lurking spy." Of course, we had also fallen a few months behind in paying our rent, which was the main reason we moved three or four times a year.

"This time it's going to work out," my mother claimed happily as we drove on. "This time it's going to *really* work out! This will be a home of our own! I won't have to drag my poor children all over the place!"

"Great, Mom," Betty said, giving me a wink.

"Terrific, Mom," I chimed in, rolling my eyes upward.

"Yes, kids! We'll have a home of our own, with nobody to tell us what to do! Nobody! It'll be *Heaven*!"

CHAPTER TWO

The Day
It Rained
Cockroaches

The three of us were very excited when we pulled
up in front of our new home. There were some
unusual things about it, but I've always been at-
tracted to unusual things. For instance, I was the
only kid I knew who always liked searching newspapers to find weird news. Whenever I found a
shocking article or picture, I'd save it. That week
alone, I had cut out a picture of a man who was
born with monkey feet, a list of Seventy-Five
Ways to Be Richer a Year from Now, and a report
about a mother who sold her daughter to Gypsies
in exchange for a theater trip to London. Also,
there are ten biographical points about me you

should know right off the bat:

1) My father ran away with one of his girlfriends when I was two years old.
2) My sister taught me how to cut out fake coins from cardboard and make imitation lamb chops out of clay, because we never had very much real money or food.
3) I once wanted to be Batman and fly off buildings.
4) I yearned to be kidnapped by aliens for a ride in their flying saucer.
5) Ever since I could remember I'd liked to make cyclorama displays out of shoeboxes and cut out figures of ghosts, beasts, and teenagers to put in them.
6) I once prayed to own a pet gorilla.
7) I used to like to play tricks on people, like putting thumbtacks on their seats.
8) When my father's father was sixteen, he got a job on a Dutch freighter, sailed to America, jumped ship and swam to Staten Island, got married, and opened a bake shop, and he and his wife died from eating too many crumbcakes before Betty and I could meet them.
9) A truck once ran over my left elbow. It really

hurt and left a little scar.
10) I am afraid I will one day die by shark attack.

About anything else you'd ever want to know
about my preteen existence you can see in the
photos in this book. However, I don't think life
really started for me until I became a teenager and
my mother moved us to Travis, on Staten Island.

When we first drove into the town, I noticed a
lot of plain wood houses, a Catholic church, a war
memorial, three saloons with men sitting outside
on chairs, seventeen women wearing kerchiefs
on their heads, a one-engine firehouse, a big red-
brick school, a candy store, and a butcher shop
with about 300 sausages hanging in the window.
Betty shot me a private look, signaling she was
aghast. Travis was mainly a Polish town, and was
so special-looking that, years later, it was picked as
a location for filming the movie *Splendor in the Grass*,
which starred Natalie Wood (before she
drowned), and Warren Beatty (before he dated
Madonna). Travis was selected because they
needed a town that looked like it was Kansas in
1920, which it still looks like.

The address of our new home was 123 Glen

Street. We stopped in front, and for a few moments the house looked normal: brown shingles, pea-soup-green–painted sides, a tiny yellow porch, untrimmed hedges, and a rickety wood gate and fence. Across the street to the left was a slope with worn gravestones all over it. The best-preserved ones were at the top, peeking out of patches of poison oak.

The backyard of our house was an airport. I mean, the house had two acres of land of its own, but beyond the rear fence was a huge field consisting of a single dirt runway, lots of old propeller-driven Piper Cub–type planes, and a cluster of rusted hangars. This was the most underprivileged airport I'd ever seen, bordered on its west side by the Arthur Kill channel and on its south side by a Con Edison electric power plant with big black mountains of coal. The only great sight was a huge apple tree on the far left corner of our property. Its trunk was at least three feet wide. It had strong, thick branches rich with new, flapping leaves. It reached upward like a giant's hand grabbing for the sky.

"Isn't everything beautiful?" Mother beamed.

"Yes, Mom," I said.

Betty gave me a pinch for lying.

"I'll plant my own rose garden," Mother went on, fumbling for the key. "Lilies, tulips, violets!"

Mom opened the front door and we went inside. We were so excited, we ran through the echoing empty rooms, pulling up old, soiled shades to let the sunlight crash in. We ran upstairs and downstairs, all over the place like wild ponies. The only unpleasant thing, from my point of view, was that we weren't the only ones running around. There were a lot of cockroaches scurrying from our invading footfalls and the shafts of light.

"Yes, the house has a few roaches," Mother confessed. "We'll get rid of them in no time!"

"How?" Betty asked raising an eyebrow.

"I bought eight Gulf Insect Bombs!"

"Where are they?" I asked.

Mother dashed out to the car and came back with one of the suitcases. From it she spilled the bombs, which looked like big silver hand grenades.

"We just put one in each room and turn them on!" Mother explained.

She took one of the bombs, set it in the middle of the upstairs kitchen, and turned on its nozzle. A cloud of gas began to stream from it, and we hurried into the other rooms to set off the other bombs.

"There!" Mother said. "Now we have to get out!"

"Get out?" I coughed.

"Yes. We must let the poison fill the house for four hours before we can come back in! Lucky for us there's a Lassie double feature playing at the Ritz!"

We hadn't been in the house ten minutes before we were driving off again!

I suppose you might as well know now that my mother really *loved* Lassie movies. The only thing she enjoyed more were movies in which romantic couples got killed at the end by tidal waves, volcanos, or other natural disasters. Anyway, I was glad we were gassing the roaches, because they are the one insect I despise. Tarantulas I like. Scorpions I can live with. But ever since I was three years old and my mother took me to a World's Fair, I have had nightmares about cockroaches. Most people remember an exciting water ride this fair had called the Shoot-the-Chutes, but emblazoned on my brain is the display the fair featured of giant, live African cockroaches, which look like American cockroaches except they're six inches long, have furry legs, and can pinch flesh. In my nightmares about them, I'm usually lying on a bed in a dark room and I notice a bevy of giant cockroaches heading for me. I try to run away but find out that someone has secretly tied me down on the bed, and the African roaches start crawling up the sides of the sheets. They walk all over my body, and then they head for my face. When they start trying to drink from my mouth is when I wake up screaming.

So after the movie I was actually looking forward to going back to the house and seeing all the dead cockroaches.

"Wasn't Lassie wonderful?" Mother sighed as she drove us back to Travis. "The way that brave dog was able to crawl hundreds of miles home after being kidnapped and beaten by Nazi Secret Service Police!"

"Yes, Mom," I agreed, although I was truthfully tired of seeing a dog movie star keep pulling the same set of tear-jerking stunts in each of its movies.

"Maybe we'll get a dog just like Lassie one day," Mother sighed.

When we got back to the house this time, we didn't run into it. We walked inside very slowly, sniffing for the deadly gas. I didn't care about the gas so much as I wanted to see a lot of roach corpses all over the place so I'd be able to sleep in peace.

But there were none.

"Where are all the dead roaches?" I asked.

"I don't know," Mother admitted.

We crept slowly upstairs to see if the bodies might be there. I knew the kitchen had the most roaches, but when we went in, I didn't see a single one, living or dead. The lone empty Gulf Insect Bomb sat spent in the middle of the floor. My sister picked up the bomb and started reading the directions. One thing my mother never did was follow directions. As Betty was reading, I noticed a closed closet door and reached out to turn its knob.

"It says here we should've opened all the closet doors before setting off the bombs, so roaches can't hide." Betty moaned, her clue to me that Mom had messed up again.

I had already started to open the door. My mind knew what was going to happen, but it was too late to tell my hand to stop pulling on the door. It sprang open, and suddenly 5,000 very angry, living cockroaches rained down on me from the ceiling of the closet.

"Eeehhhhhh!" I screamed, leaping around the

room, bathed in bugs, slapping at the roaches crawling all over me and down my neck! "Eeehhh-hhh! Eeehh! Ehhh! Ehh!"

"Don't worry. I'll get more bombs," Mother said comfortingly as she grabbed an old dishrag to knock the fluttering roaches off my back. Betty calmly reached out her foot to crunch as many as dared run by her.

CHAPTER THREE

How the Pigman's Daughter Came into Our Lives

Actually the most preposterous thing I witnessed that year of Travis was that my mother had arranged to *buy*, not rent, the house in Travis. You would do well to wonder how my mom was able to buy a house when we were broke most of the time, but what Mother lacked in money, she made up for in being able to talk a mile a minute. A lot of people liked her gift of gab, and several used to ask her advice about a lot of things, and she'd always make believe she knew what she was talking about. In this world it doesn't seem to matter if you know anything as long as you *pretend* to know it.

One of the people who came to Mom for help was Connie Vivona, the daughter of Nonno Frankie, my pigman-to-be. Truth is stranger than fiction, so brace yourself while I tell you how my mother met Connie Vivona.

Connie Vivona showed up at our last apartment crying and holding the hands of her identical-twin sons, Nicky and Joey. Connie was simply walking the streets crying and ringing strangers' doorbells because her husband had abandoned her and his two sons, and she was about to lose her mind. Her husband had gone to Las Vegas one night, decided he'd had enough of her and the twins, divorced her, and taken off to live in Paris.

So one morning our doorbell rang. Mom peeked out from behind the faded lace curtains and opened the door, and there stood this plump, cute, young Italian woman with makeup and two kids.

"Oh, God!" The woman broke down crying, straightening her red knit dress. "I have no place to live!"

I know this is hard to believe, but my mother let this complete stranger in and told me to go play with the twins while she listened to Connie Vivona's entire life story. And let me tell you, Nicky and Joey were very strange twins. They were zesty kids, five years younger than me, and they loved to do crazy things. They both had handsome little olive faces, springy black hair, and big eyes like trusting raccoons'. The craziest thing I told them to do that afternoon was to crawl down a flight of stairs headfirst. And they did it! If you've never tried it, you really should. It's quite an experience at any age. Then, after the stairs, I told them to spin around in circles, which they did until they dropped. Then I told them to catch squirrels in the backyard. I really liked Nicky and Joey, though I couldn't tell one from the other. They loved everything I told them to do. They laughed and puffed, and even that very first day I could tell they looked up to me with enormous respect.

And Mother and Connie got along great, particularly when Mother found out Connie had over $800 in a bank account.

"There's so much you can do with eight hundred dollars," my mother joyously told her. "So much *we* can do."

What Mom finally got Connie to do was buy

the house in Travis with $500 down. Even though the money was Connie's, Mom explained that her own business expertise represented an equal contribution, so they signed the mortgage papers as *co-owners* of the house. The whole setup was so complicated it gave me a teenage headache, but the important parts you have to know are as follows:

a) Connie and her twins were due to move in the day after us. They had gone to Manhattan to pick up some of their belongings, which they had stored with her mother and father, Nonna Mamie and Nonno Frankie.

b) Nonna and Nonno mean "Grandmother" and "Grandfather" in Italian.

c) I had no idea then that Nonno Frankie would turn out to be my pigman.

d) Nonna Mamie and Nonno Frankie had fled Italy because they hated its dictator, Benito Mussolini. A lot of Italians loved Mussolini in the beginning, but after a while they caught on to his character defects and knocked him off.

e) Nonna Mamie and Nonno Frankie were gainfully employed at NBC in Manhattan. I thought that meant they were working at the National Broadcasting Company, but it turned out their NBC meant the National Biscuit Company. Nonno Frankie's job was to help load batter into giant mixing bowls, and Nonna Mamie's job was to stand at one side of a block-long conveyor belt and remove imperfect Oreo cookies before they traveled on to the packaging machines.

Anyway, somehow it was worked out that my mother, sister, and I would live upstairs in the Travis house, and Connie and the twins would live downstairs. They would split the mortgage payments, which were around $150 a month, a lot of money then.

Now that first day, after the attack of the angry cockroaches, I just wanted to get a breath of fresh air, so I decided to go out the front gate and see if there were any signs of life on Glen Street. To my surprise there was a girl my age jumping rope in front of our house. She was a pretty girl, with rosy-red cheeks, and she had nice shiny brown hair that flopped when she jumped.

"Hi," she said, still jumping rope. "I'm Jennifer Wolupopski. I live three doors up."

"Hi," I said.

"You just move in?"

"Yes."

"What's your name?"

"Paul Zindel," I said.

"Are you Polish?" she wanted to know, continuing to bob up and down.

"Actually, no."

"I am."

Jennifer stopped jumping and strolled over to me. "Have you seen the water-head baby yet?" she asked.

"The what?"

"The water-head baby."

"No."

She pointed to a maroon house next door. A young black woman sat in front on a bench. She gently rocked a baby carriage that had a white veil draped over its hood.

"You live next to the only colored families in town, you know," Jennifer said.

"No, I didn't know," I admitted.

"Everyone else is Polish. You want to see the water-head baby?"

"O.K."

She marched me toward the baby carriage.

"Hi, Mrs. Lillah," Jennifer called out to the black woman. "This is Paul, one of your new neighbors."

Mrs. Lillah smiled, cooling herself with a Japanese fan. She was a fascinatingly delicate woman who kept lovingly rocking the veiled carriage. I began chatting with her, but I was afraid to look down into the carriage. I didn't want it to look like I had strolled over only to see her water-head baby. Besides, I had never even heard of a water-head baby, much less seen one. I kept my eyes glued to Mrs. Lillah, telling her about my mother and sister. I also explained that an Italian woman with identical twins would soon be moving in, too. Meanwhile, Jennifer stood behind Mrs. Lillah and kept signalling me to look into the carriage. Finally, Mrs. Lillah turned to swat a fly and I did take a quick look down. There, beyond the veil, was the baby. Its tiny body looked like that of a normal six-month-old, but attached to the body was a head the size of a watermelon with the texture of glistening cauliflower. I gasped at the sight of the huge head, with its tiny wet eyes and practically no nose or chin. The baby's skull was twice the size of its entire body, and it gasped like a fish out of water. I felt my knees grow weak.

"Hope you're gonna like livin' 'round here," Mrs.

Lillah said, lifting the veil and reaching into the carriage to gently stroke her baby's tummy.

"I'm sure I will."

"See you later, Mrs. Lillah," Jennifer said, taking my arm and leading me quickly away.

When we were out of sight behind the hedge, I started to gag. Jennifer began to laugh nervously. I know this'll sound horrible, but after a while my gagging turned to laughing, too. And I knew Jennifer and I weren't laughing to be cruel. It was simply the only way we could handle coming face to face with one of God's mysteries. I mean, we laughed and laughed out of fright until I knew I had found a new friend and kindred spirit in Jennifer Wolupopski. In fact, that afternoon she took me all along Glen Street and Victory Boulevard and pointed out the important sights. She told me the old abandoned graveyard was called "Cemetery Hill" and was great for sled riding in the winter as long as you didn't crash into one of the tombstones.

Suddenly, there was a VAAAAARRRRROOO-OOOOM! A plane took off right over our heads, nearly splitting our eardrums.

"That's a BT-6 Basic Trainer," Jennifer said.

"How do you know?"

How the Pigman's Daughter Came into Our Lives

"Oh, you'll know every plane from the airport soon enough. You know, I bet we'll be in a lot of the same classes when school starts."

"I hope so," I said.

Suddenly the excitement in Jennifer's eyes turned to concern.

"The other boys are really going to not like you in this town, you know," she said.

"Why?"

"Because you're not Polish. And because you have blond hair. And because you're new. Some of the boys'll try to work you over."

"What'll they do?"

"Rotten things. They always think of rotten things. They'll also not like you because you live next to the town's only colored families. The kids in the town are really demented, you know. The worst is Moose Kaminski, who lives over there." She pointed to a large gray house far on the other side of Cemetery Hill. "Moose's whole family are lunatics. His brothers. His mother. His father. Sometimes they stick strange parts of their bodies out the upstairs windows when you walk by. I think they're genetically defective. Of course, some of the families who live here have never even been off Staten Island. Never even taken the ferryboat to Manhattan. All most of them do is sit around drinking beer, eating sausages, and dancing the polka."

"What kind of dance is that?"

"It's like a waltz, but at high speed. And a lot of the Polish guys get drunk at St. Anthony's Parish Hall dances on Saturday nights."

"There's got to be some *nice* Polish people in town."

"Oh, most of them are. But those you don't have to worry about. I'm just warning you about the teenage fiends."

"That's really nice of you."

"That's O.K.," Jennifer said. "I'd really like to be your friend," she added.

"Thank you," I said. "I need a friend. I'll be your friend, too."

When I finally went back home, Mother had already unpacked everything and was playing her phonograph. She was in our kitchen dancing and singing along to an Andrews Sisters record when I came up the stairs.

"Hello, my baby!" she sang. *"Hello, my honey! Hello, my ragtime gal. Send me a kiss by wire! Baby, my heart's on fire."*

She pranced. Did some boogie-woogie steps. I

remember hoping she would never be depressed or threaten to kill herself ever again, but that stuff I'll tell you about later. Of course, I also hoped seeing a water-head baby would be the only ghastly thing that would happen to me in the town of Travis.

But no way. *No way!*

CHAPTER FOUR

The Day I Learned the Beauty of Worms

Early the next morning, my mother started laying down a lot of rules about the house for me and my sister. She wanted us pretty well regimented before Connie and the twins arrived. The major rule was that we were to respect Connie's privacy and shouldn't hang out in the downstairs apartment, except for one room, the "side room," which my mother had claimed as "our territory" because it had a Pianola in it. A Pianola is a piano that you can play the regular way or put a special roll in it and pump it with your feet so it plays songs like "The Hungarian Rhapsody" without you using your fingers.

"Don't go into Connie's rooms," Mother said. "Then her two wild little brats won't feel free to come upstairs and rampage through our rooms."

That was the one thing that used to drive me nuts about Mom. She always made up hundreds of rules. My sister and I sometimes felt like helpless puppets on strings. Also, that morning she had us move around a few beds and other pieces of junky furniture she had bought with the house. My sister and I each had a lumpy bed in our upstairs front rooms. Mom had a double bed in the rear, and we had a peeling, brown kitchenette set in our upstairs kitchen. I'd better draw you a map of the layout, because the house and yard got to play a very big role in all our lives.

At 11 A.M. a Sabatini Brothers moving van pulled up and stopped in front of our house. This was not a modern moving van. It was old, came with two moving men who looked like they had just escaped from *The Lost World*, and boasted a sign that said "Cheap Rates." It was an open-top truck piled high with Connie Vivona's furniture, in addition to a considerable amount of human cargo.

OUR HOUSE IN TRAVIS

LEGEND of where things were:
1. The beautiful apple tree
2. My room and lumpy bed
3. My sister's room
4. My mother's room
5. The upstairs kitchen where the cockroaches attacked me
6. The 'SIDE ROOM'
7. A junky garage used for junk
8. A fairly good tool shed
9. Our ~~~~ acre to run around in
10. Connie Vivona's ~~~ acre to run around in
11. Connie's downstairs apartment
12. The black family's house
13. The spot where I met Mrs. Lillah and her water-head baby
14. Jennifer Wolupopski's residence
15. Cemetery Hill
16. The underprivileged airport

The Day I Learned the Beauty of Worms

Connie, in a purple dress, and her twins, Joey and Nicky, climbed out of the back along with one of the hairy moving men. The other moving man got out from behind the wheel of the truck, loped around, and opened the passenger side. At first, all I could see was a wall of shopping bags, but then a little old lady, who turned out to be Nonna Mamie, got out. The last one to get out was Nonno Frankie. He was a little on the short side and had a bit of a pot belly and eyes that danced, like a Sicilian Santa Claus. I figured he was at least fifty years old but better preserved than Nonna Mamie.

Connie introduced her mother and father to us. The twins immediately began running around like matching mice, jumping over the fence and swinging on the porch poles. The Sabatini Brothers started unloading the truck and checking the best way to get all the furniture and packing boxes into the house. Connie had beds and wooden bureaus and big nightstands and at least thirty cartons of clothes and kitchen items. None of the furniture looked custom-made or anything like that. It was more like the kind you saw in advertisements offering three full rooms of furniture for $99. Of course, it was elegant compared to anything we had ever had, but everything was gold or scarlet or bright pink with weird tassels and gizmos swinging from it.

It didn't take long before everyone had said "Hello." When Nonna Mamie put her arms around me to give me a hug, I realized she was a dwarf. I mean, she wasn't quite a full-fledged dwarf, but she was a very tiny lady whose feet looked like they could've fit into a pair of Tom Thumb's boots, which I had seen on display at Barnum's Circus Hall of Curiosities. Right off the bat, she hit the downstairs kitchen and started sprinkling cleanser into the sink, mopping the floor, and shooting orders to the Sabatini Brothers about where to put all the pots and pans and boxes. Almost everything she said was in Italian, but you could tell she was a friendly, hard-working old lady.

Soon, my mother put on a how-dare-you-trespass look on her face and shot it straight at me and my sister. Betty groaned, gave me a wink, and headed upstairs. I ran out into the backyard. To my surprise, Nonno Frankie followed me out.

I'll never forget the expression on his face when he saw the big backyard. He looked like he had died and gone to heaven.

"What a place to grow tomatoes!" he cried out.

"Yes, sir," I agreed, though I had never planted a living thing in my life.

He knelt down and grabbed a handful of dirt. "I'll plant tomatoes! And eggplants! And corn and rhubarb and carrots!"

He stood up, sniffed at the earth in his hands, then breathed in deeply like he was sampling a French perfume. He began checking out every square inch of the backyard. His billowing plaid shirt flickered against his belly, and he wore brown baggy pants like a clown's. Excited, he talked a mile a minute.

"You like meatballs?"

"Yes, sir."

"Good. Nonna Mamie makes meatballs so good and spicy, they'll blow your ears off. You like vegetables?"

"Not really, sir."

"Ho! Ho! Ho!" he laughed, giving me a wink. "Don't clean your plate!—don't get any dessert! You like carrots?"

"Yes, sir."

"Good. Then all you have to remember are the three B's."

"What three B's?"

"Be careful, Be good, and Be home early!" He

laughed so heartily I thought he was going to tumble over. He stooped to snatch another handful of dirt near the remains of a grape arbor, which divided the backyard exactly in half. I knew there'd be a problem.

"THAT'S MY HALF OF THE YARD! WOULD YOU MIND KEEPING ON CONNIE'S HALF?" my mother screamed from her upstairs back window.

Nonno Frankie whirled to see Mom hanging half out the window, motioning that he was to keep on the territory to the right side of the arbor.

"Okay Dokay!" Nonno Frankie laughed, waving that he understood. He shuffled like a good little old man back to Connie's side, still happy as a lark, and started pulling up weeds.

"Do you know why you should never tell a secret to a pig?" he asked me out of the blue.

"No, I don't, sir," I admitted.

"Because they're *squealers!*" He laughed loudly.

"That's very funny," I said.

"And did you see that graveyard across the street?" he asked, his eyes twinkling.

"Yes, sir."

"I wouldn't be caught dead there. *Do you get it?* I wouldn't be caught *dead* there!"

"Yes, sir." I laughed. "I *get* it."

He strolled onward, with me right behind him. "Look at *this*!" he gasped, pulling a cluster of long, pink, wiggling bodies from a clump of moist earth. "Worms! Hardworking worms! Worms are in only the best dirt! The very best! Worms in a yard are a dream come true. A miracle! What tomatoes they will give us! What tomatoes!"

"PAUL!" My mother screamed from the upstairs window again. "STOP PESTERING NONNO FRANKIE AND GET BACK ON YOUR OWN SIDE OF THE YARD! GET OVER THERE IM-MEDIATELY, PAUL!"

I cringed.

"He's not bothering me," Nonno Frankie called back to her. "He's a good boy. A good boy!"

"PAUL, JUST DO AS I SAID! DO IT NOW!" my mother shrieked, slamming the window closed.

I started to walk away. Nonno Frankie sighed and looked at me so kindly, I knew he understood I had a slightly wacko person for a mom.

CHAPTER FIVE

An Unexpected Dinner

As I've already hinted, my mother wasn't completely nuts. She had positive traits, like being pretty and energetic. She could let out a good loud laugh from time to time, had a lot of dreams and schemes, and had beautiful brown darting eyes and bouncy hair like a flapper's. On the other hand, because of my father's divorcing her and other sundry reasons, she was a man-hater, didn't know how to love, couldn't cook, didn't care for housework, and didn't join social groups and neighborhood coffee sessions because she thought people wanted to spy on her.

The only man my mother had really loved had

been her father. He was an Irish man who married a lovely Irish woman, who gave birth to my mom. Mom's mother died when she was fifteen, so Mom had to be raised by her father, a gentle, skinny man who hawked fruits and vegetables from a horse-drawn cart. Mother and her dad used to ride together through the streets of Stapleton singing songs about vegetables at the top of their lungs. "APPLES! PEARS! FRESH CUCUMBERS!" Sometimes they'd get down and dance around the wagon, ringing bells in the street. Anything to attract attention to sell their wares.

Mother told me only two stories about her growing up. The first one was about the day she took the horse and wagon without telling her father and gave all her teenage friends a big, long joyride. The second story was more hair-raising. It concerned a doll salesman who rented a room in her dad's dilapidated old brown house on Grove Street. The salesman rented the room only to store hundreds of magnificent dolls in it. Each was wrapped separately in a casket-shaped box with a cellophane window, and the salesman would take only a few dozen or so with him when he'd go on selling trips to towns between Boston and Atlantic City. Mother desperately wanted one of the expensive dolls, but all she was allowed to do was go outside the house and stand on a milk crate to peer through the window at the tiny frozen faces staring back at her. Each of the dolls was identical, about two feet tall, with gorgeous platinum-blond hair, glowing white porcelain skin, delicate expressive fingers with painted red nails, and deep-blue imitation star sapphires for eyes.

A day finally came when my mother's dream to own one of the dolls came true. What happened was the doll salesman didn't come back for over a year, and was so far behind in his rent that Mom's father broke the padlock on the door and gave her one of the dolls. Mother said she grabbed the box, ran to her room, and trembled with excitement as she lifted out the doll. She felt as though she had paradise within her grasp. But as she went to hug the doll, its wig fell off, leaving the doll completely bald except for a massive colony of wiggling and very surprised maggots that were eating the glue on the doll's head. Mom's dad had to throw out all the dolls. He was really going to give the salesman a piece of his mind, but the man never returned.

Anyway, when Mother was sixteen, she started dating my father, the baker's son. There's a picture of them I cherish because my mother and father have their arms around each other, and they look like a very loving couple out of an extremely emotional movie based on a novel like *The Grapes of Wrath.* Mother has on a blouse and nice hat, and my father looks strong and ready to protect her like the high school football hero he was. According to Mother, however, she and my father got married only because her dad got TB and on his deathbed he squeezed her hand and said, "Please get married before I die." Since he only had a few weeks left to live, that didn't leave much time, so my mom and pop became husband and wife when they were in their late teens. Within a year, Mom gave birth to Betty, and two years later I was born, just in time, because my mother and father were already heading for a divorce. My father had changed professions, had graduated from Police Academy to become a New York City policeman. He had to commute to work in Manhattan. He also graduated to having girlfriends on the sly. My mother found out about his girlfriends and divorced him, and that was the end of her having a husband and me having a father.

Now I can get on to the shocking part of this flashback, which has to do with screaming and opening windows. That part happened when I was four years old and my sister was six, and we had a fight over a bowl of Campbell's chicken noodle soup. Betty and I were sitting at the kitchen table in our tiny apartment while my mother was getting dressed to go to work. She earned about twenty-five cents an hour at a women's stockings and garters factory. My sister was teasing me, pretending she was going to sneak a tablespoon of boring chicken soup from her bowl into my bowl.

"Mama, Betty put a spoonful of soup into my bowl!" I lied.

"I did not!" Betty complained. "I only *made believe* I was going to!"

"She did, Mom! She did!" I kept bellyaching.

I think it was exactly at that moment my mother went really wacko for the first time.

"I can't take it anymore!" she suddenly screamed. "I'm going to kill myself!"

"No, Mama! No!" Betty and I pleaded. We ran around the room after her, but she put on her coat.

"I'm going out to jump off a bridge!" Mother said.

I cried and cried, and we both pulled at her coat to stop her, but she smacked us away. "I hate life! I hate getting stuck with you two stones around my neck! I hate the way you rotten kids fight! I hate everything, so I'm going to leap headfirst off the Bayonne Bridge!"

I wailed still more, pleaded, but she brushed me away, went out, and slammed the door. Betty and I ran to the front window. Our apartment was on the second floor, and we had a good view of Mom as she walked across the street to wait at the bus stop.

"She'll be back," Betty said, suddenly very factual, comforting me. She often had to act as emergency babysitter.

I threw open the window, leaned out, and cried to Mom.

"PLEASE DON'T KILL YOURSELF! PLEASE DON'T," I wept.

"IT'S TOO LATE! I'VE HAD ENOUGH! THE BAYONNE BRIDGE IS THREE HUNDRED FEET HIGH!" she yelled. "I'LL BE DEAD WHEN I HIT THE WATER!"

"NO, MAMA! NO!"

"YES!"

"NO!"

"IF I'M NOT KILLED IN THE PLUNGE, I'LL DROWN IN THE UNDERTOW!" Mother added. "GOOD-BYE YOU UNGRATEFUL CHIL-

DREN! GOOD-BYE!"

Betty didn't look very worried, but I felt my heart was ready to break. I hung out the open window, wailing, begging. My only hope was that when the bus came, Mother would tell us she had changed her mind.

But the bus did come, and the last thing Mother called to us was "WISH ME A HAPPY SUICIDE!" Then she got on the bus and was gone.

Later that day, at her usual time after work, Mom came home. Her clothes were dry. She didn't mention anything more about hurtling herself off any bridge. She didn't even mention our treachery with the Campbell's chicken noodle soup. But my sister and I behaved ourselves for a rather long time. We were so good, in fact, that Mother didn't threaten to kill herself after that more than two or three times a year. Sometimes she'd tell us she was going to put her head in the oven and turn the gas on while we were sleeping. A few times she said she was going to run out and hurl herself in front of a speeding five-axle truck. Once she threatened to run through a park during a thunderstorm so a bolt of lightning could strike her in the head. After a while, though, my sister and I both got used to her threats.

"I don't blame Mom for thinking about suicide," Betty once told me. "The world *is* a pretty horrible place."

�֍

"Yoo hoo!" Nonno Frankie's voice floated upstairs, along with the most delicious smells of food I'd ever smelled. My mother made a face and strutted to the top of the stairs like a prison matron disturbed by an inmate.

"What do you want?" Mother called down to Nonno Frankie. Betty and I scooted to peer out from behind her.

"Dinner's ready!" Nonno Frankie beamed.

"Look, you have your kitchen down there and we have our kitchen up here." All my mother was heating up was a can of frankfurters and beans. "Don't worry about us," Mom said icily.

"No," Nonno Frankie said. "You're eating with us tonight! The table's set for all of us!"

I could tell Mom was poised to cut off her nose to spite our faces, when the house began to vibrate with a tremendous VAAAAROOOOOOOOM! The entire house shook whenever any plane took off over it.

"Hey, who invented the first airplane that *didn't*

fly?" Nonno Frankie called up.

"I don't know." Mother frowned, convinced she was speaking to an immigrant lunatic.

"The *Wrong* Brothers!" Nonno Frankie laughed.

Mom thought that over a minute. Then she actually laughed. Finally, we were all laughing at the silly joke, and I knew we'd all be having dinner together downstairs.

Against her will, my mother was excited when she went downstairs. She looked happy. She had put on lipstick and an ironed brown shiny dress. Even my sister was cheerful, brushing her long blond hair and sniffing at the air with an appetite. For me, going to a real dinner seemed like an adventure. I was the last one downstairs because I brushed my teeth and combed my hair flat so it didn't look like an unkempt carrottop.

At sunset, the front hallway was dark and shadowy. The stairs creaked as I crept down alone. There was a naked bulb swinging in a draft near the front door. Farther down the hall it got much darker and more shadowy. To get into Connie Vivona's apartment, I had to walk into a small dark storeroom, which appeared like a gaping monster's mouth at the far end.

The door was open. I went in. Around a little

My grandmother and grandfather on my father's side of the family. I never met them because they were dead by the time I was born. His name was Eugene, which is my middle name. Her name was Pauline. They fell in love, opened a bakery, and made crumb buns.

My mother as a young girl. She looks so sweet and innocent to me, and I wonder why God let Life work her over so much.

My mother and father are on the right as the bridesmaid and best man at somebody's wedding. I wish marriages could last forever, or at least until the kids are thirty-three.

This is my father, who
became a New York
City cop, met a
girlfriend, and left us.
I wish I had known
him better.

This is my favorite picture of my mother
and father. I dedicated my first novel,
The Pigman, to them, calling them
"The Boy and Girl from Stapleton."

Me, my mother, and my
sister. I'm the one all wrapped
up like a baby mummy.

*My mother when she was still a
normal, loving mother and wife.*

Betty and me.

My sister Betty and me. I think I look like an extraterrestrial in this photo.

Me, my mother, my sister, and a dog whose name I can't remember. This photo was taken just before my mother and father called it splitsville.

Betty and me sitting on a running board, which cars don't have anymore.

My favorite picture of my sister.

bend I could see Connie's bedroom. Just the sight of her bed gave me a fright. It was shockingly gussied up by a bedspread with a design of giant roses all over it. Eight bizarre Kewpie dolls were reclining against a bunch of loud, flowery pillows, and all the dolls were staring at me. They had little white faces, two inches wide. These dolls were freaky, healthy-looking dolls, with huge crocheted hats and dresses that fanned out into large rainbow circles—not the kind of dolls with rotting wigs like my mother's.

I stared at the dolls like I'd been paralyzed by a black widow spider's bite. The storeroom also had a pocket of chilly air, which made me think a ghoul might be living in it. I knew something horrible had happened in that storeroom, or that one day something awful *would* happen there. And as it would turn out, I was right.

I shook off the premonition and walked out through Connie's bedroom. Along the way I saw nice things:

1) There were curtains, tablecloths, slipcovers on chairs, lampshades, Venice painted on velvet, and a pretty fringed orange throw rug. Connie and her parents had clearly been

working all day and had fixed up the apartment so it looked like civilized people resided there.

2) Connie's closet door was open, and I glimpsed a few dresses with sequins and feathers, three pairs of high-heeled fancy shoes, embroidered sweaters, and a bottle of Evening in Paris perfume. Preliminary evidence suggested Connie was *not* a man-hater.

3) There was a small Singer sewing machine.

4) A radio playing Frank Sinatra singing "I Get a Kick out of You" was sitting on a night table.

5) The twins' room in the front was decorated with Donald Duck blankets, toys, and normal children's clothes on hangers.

6) A red, blue, purple, yellow, and green beaded curtain had been put up, so when you walked through the archway to get to the kitchen, you felt as though you were entering a fancy bar in Hawaii.

7) In the kitchen, the table was set with attractive artificial camellias, red and gold cloth napkins, and dinner plates with dancing Italian peasants on them.

8) The room was toasty with a wood fire in the stove.

9) Pots of food were gurgling.
10) There was a big, long loaf of succulent-looking bread.

Most of all, I guess, I noticed happiness.

"Taste! Taste!" Nonno Frankie said, rushing at me with a plate of delicious-looking fried some-things on it.

I scooped up one of the dark, crispy squares and put it in my mouth. It was the most savory thing I'd ever chewed in my whole life.

"Watch out for the bones," Nonno Frankie warned.

"What is it?" I asked.

"Fried eel!" He beamed. "Fried baby eel!"

CHAPTER SIX

Zombies on the Porches

Nonno Frankie and Nonna Mamie had made the best meal I had ever seen or eaten on earth. Mom, Betty, me, and the twins sat around the big kitchen table while Connie and her mother and father put a breathtaking Sicilian gourmet feast before us. After the eel appetizer came large hot plates of spaghetti with shimmering lakes of tomato sauce ladled out from a ten-gallon pot bubbling on top of the stove. Nonno Frankie ran around with a big slab of Parmesan cheese, rubbing it like crazy against a metal-toothed rack. I had never seen fresh-grated cheese before.

"Ho! Ho! Ho! What's a ghost's favorite food?" he quizzed.

None of us knew.

"Spookghetti!" he howled. *"Spookghetti!"*

Everybody was laughing and eating, as lip-smacking course after lip-smacking course hit the table. There was Italian ham with wedges of fresh mozzarella, anchovies and tomatoes with oil, vinegar, and exotic herbs. There were fat green olives and steaming garlic bread. And just when any ordinary meal would have been over, out of the oven came the main event: a deep, hot pan with luscious pork chops, browned sausages, plump zesty chicken breasts, thighs, necks, and legs. There were so many shiny, undulating delicious things floating about, the scent made me nearly faint. Along with the meats, Nonno Frankie served a dark, blood-red wine from a straw-covered bottle.

"It'll grow hair on your chest," he said, laughing, giving even little Nicky and Joey each a small glass, which they chugalugged like seasoned imbibers. As usual, the twins didn't sit still for long. They stuffed their faces and went dashing around the house to play some more.

"They run around too much," Nonno Frankie said.

"They're just kids," Connie reminded him.

"They should walk, and not yell so much!"

I could tell the twins got on Nonno Frankie's nerves a little, but he'd give them candies and hugs from time to time so they knew he really loved them.

"I can't wait until they get to be grown-up like you," Nonno Frankie whispered to me. That made me feel good.

After the main course came the desserts: lemon sherbet, cannolis, which are tubular crusts stuffed with cream, cassata rum cake, cookies with rainbow sprinkles on them, chocolate-covered nuts, Stella D'oro crisps, espresso coffee, a shot of almond liqueur, and a big bowl of pears, grapes, berries, oranges, and figs. The whole meal took over three hours to eat, but there was a lot of sophisticated, titillating conversation as well. Topics covered were B-17 bombers, the Brooklyn Dodgers, Sir Winston Churchill, bobbysoxers' fashions, slumber parties, imbecilic, moronic screaming-meemie autograph fans at Frank Sinatra concerts, Nazi spies, the price of nylons, the glory of worms, and the importance of a good virgin olive oil.

The one who turned out to have a great sense of humor, besides Nonno Frankie, was Connie. She was sweet and generous. She had made her face up with lipstick, rouge, and eyebrow pencil so she looked very fetching and hardly plump. She was much happier than when she had first knocked on our old apartment door in tears. Connie mostly made a lot of jokes and comments about men and what awful husbands she and my mother had gotten stuck with, and my mother laughed a lot. After a second glass of wine, Mom even agreed to do the one imitation she knew, which was to laugh like a wild witch. She usually only performed that around Halloween, but Betty and I urged her on after dinner because we knew her "witch laugh" was surefire to warm up any party. When she let out her first loud, two-minute cackle, even the twins stood still, their big dark eyes wide open in amazement. Then they pleaded for Mother to do eight encores of her witch laugh.

The only part my mother didn't enjoy about Connie's humor was when Connie occasionally blurted out, "Oh, he can park his shoes under my bed anytime!" Connie said this almost every time the name of any male star came up, including Clark Gable, Laurence Olivier, Rudolph Valentino, Enrico Caruso, and Roy Rogers.

It was a meal to remember, and when Nonno Frankie and Nonna Mamie departed on Sunday, they left lots of food for Connie to share with us during the week.

"You know how to tell twin witches apart?" Nonno Frankie whispered to me in farewell.

"No," I said.

"Well, it's not easy to tell which witch is which! Ho! Ho! Ho!" He winked, grabbed Nonna Mamie's hand, and hobbled off with her to catch the #112 bus back to Manhattan.

※

By Tuesday, I missed Nonno Frankie.

Everything was too quiet with him gone, but Jennifer stopped over and asked if I felt like taking a walk.

"Sure," I said.

First we strolled up Glen Street, and I told her all about the meal, Connie's decor, and Nonno Frankie.

"I'd really like to meet him," she said, tossing her shiny brown hair all to the left side of her face. It made her look very pretty in an unusual sort of way.

"I'll introduce you next weekend," I promised.

"Great."

Then we stopped at Jennifer's house. She wanted me to meet her mother and father, who were sitting on rocking chairs out on the porch.

"This is Paul," Jennifer told them.

"Hello, Mr. Wolupopski," I said. "Hello, Mrs. Wolupopski."

They smiled from their chairs and nodded. They both had white hair and looked like their idea of a good time was to sit all day on the porch and count the tombstones across the street on Cemetery Hill. Jennifer looked very embarrassed, and she got me out of there real quick. We continued up the street.

"They're ancient, aren't they?" Jennifer said.

"They seem nice," I said.

"You don't have to kid me," Jennifer said, looking down at the ground. Her hair fell back to frame her face. "I know they're zombies. My mother didn't give birth to me until she was fifty-three."

"Why'd she wait so long?"

"She was busy having my eleven brothers."

"You have eleven brothers?"

"None of them live at home."

"Where are they?"

"Oh, they're married with kids of their own. A lot of them work across the Arthur Kill at factories like the American Cyanamid Company and U.S. Metals. I got left home with the two zombies." The sad way her eyes looked toward the river made me feel depressed.

"Your parents look O.K."

"O.K., but drained. A lot of the parents in this town look just like them. They pop out kids all their lives and then retire to sit on their porches." She sighed deeply.

Jennifer pointed out other houses, and sure enough, a lot had a pair of pleasant-looking mother and father zombie duos on them. They had neat, civilized, earth-colored pants, skirts, kerchiefs, and sweaters on, and most had full shocks of white hair.

"Half of them only know a little English," Jennifer said. "They're ashamed to speak to anyone who isn't Polish. They make all of their teenaged kids deranged. All the young boys go really nuts until they can flee this place. I warned you they'll be mean to you when school starts. You'll see about that soon enough."

I was glad I had the whole summer ahead of me before then.

Then Jennifer pointed out two houses with normal families. One had a nice teenage girl called Jeanette Filopowicz in it, and she had a colorful family with a lot of older, dynamic married brothers who Jennifer said had good hearts. Jennifer also told me about the Matusiewitz family, who had lovely daughters, one of whom could play the first ten bars of Tchaikovsky's Piano Concerto No. 1, and sons who were supposed to have become loving, fine fathers. But a lot of the other porches had rocking parent zombies on them.

When we got back from our stroll, I suggested we hang out at the stupendously big apple tree in the back of my yard. On closer inspection the tree was even more appealing, because I realized my nosy mother with her eagle eyes couldn't see us there. The toolshed and a few other trees blocked her view from both the upstairs kitchen and bedroom windows.

We sat down on the ground and leaned against the tree, and I started filling Jennifer in on a few of the weirder details about my own mother so she wouldn't feel so bad about her zombie parents, but the twins came running out, scooting in circles around us, until I invented a game I called "let's jump out of the apple tree!" Jennifer and I just sat and conversed while I told the twins to climb the tree and see how high they could leap from. The first jump they made was from about three feet. They jumped from there for about ten minutes. Then I told them they should climb higher so it'd be even more fun to jump. They got as high as about ten feet and kept jumping, climbing, and jumping, landing in a pile of dried weeds. They were good kids, but I really wanted to be alone with Jennifer for a while. I finally told them to see how many other things they could find to jump off in the whole yard. They liked that idea and dashed off out of our sight.

They weren't gone a minute when Jennifer and I decided *we* should climb the tree and sit up in it awhile. The tree formed a thick cradle where the trunk made its first split, five feet off the ground. It was a perfect hideout, surrounded by a lush cluster of large green leaves and branches half woven like a big nest.

"It's beautiful up here," Jennifer said. "We can see everything!"

"And no one can see us!" I added.

And it was true. We could see the whole yard, the airport, and Mrs. Lillah's house, which had the water-head baby and chickens, ducks, and rabbits in its backyard. The land was so flat we could also easily see the monstrous black oil tankers on the river, and the coal being gurgled up onto a conveyor belt at the Con Edison electric plant.

"Where's your mother today?" Jennifer wanted to know.

"She and Connie went to answer ads for work," I said. "Now that they own the house, they have to pay the mortgage."

"What kind of jobs are they looking for?"

"Mom saw a help-wanted advertisement for the ASPCA, the society to protect animals. If she gets that, she can ride around in a big van with a veterinarian and stick free needles into everybody's dogs and cats so they don't get rabies."

"That'd be exciting," Jennifer said.

"Yes," I agreed. "And Connie's gone for an interview to be a hatcheck girl at Ye Olde Tavern Lounge in New Dorp. She got all dressed up for it and said they only hire personnel who have a lot of glamor."

"My mother never went to work," Jennifer said, her voice a strange mixture of embarrassment and fear. "And my father's retired now, but he used to clean the electroplating tanks at Nassau Smelting, where they melt down junk cars to salvage metal."

"That must have been interesting."

"It wasn't." Jennifer's voice trailed off. She looked away from me, so now I knew something was really wrong.

There was a long silence.

When she looked back at me, she had tears in her eyes. It was like anything fake had melted away between us, and I was seeing her for the first time. Her cheeks were flushed, and her hair blended in with the branches. She looked like the most sensitive person I had ever met, as though her feelings were all over her outside. A weird thought jumped into my mind. A sad thought. I felt sad for Jennifer that she wasn't more beautiful. In the last school I'd gone to there was a very beautiful girl who everyone knew was going to have a wonderful life. She was invited to every party. All the boys gawked and showed off for her. She wore just a touch of something like an *eau de toilette*, some delicate fragrance that floated from her; maybe it was even manufactured by her own shoulders or in the nape of her neck. And it made me dream of holding her and disappearing into her skin. Of course, I hardly got to speak to that girl. But Jennifer looked different, more like she could one day win a minor downhill skiing championship or attempt to swim the English Channel. Her violet eyes, even with their tears, were her strongest feature. At that moment, in the apple tree, I felt I could fall into them, that I could see there was a fine beautiful soul deep inside her brain but that many boys wouldn't take the time to find it.

"What's the matter?" I asked.

"I'm going to die in this town," she said, brushing the tears from her eyes.

"What do you mean *you're going to die?*"

"I mean, I'm trapped like a muskrat. That's what all the boys do in this town. Trap muskrats and skin them alive."

"You're not trapped!"

"Yes, I am. All I'll ever know is this town. It's all any of the girls get to know when you're born here and have zombies for parents and muskrat killers for boyfriends. They make you get married before you're twenty. I'll be married and then they'll make me a baby machine, and I'll do huge washes, hang out clothes, fry kielbasa sausages, roast potatoes, mop floors, dance the polka, get fat, wrinkle, turn all white, and never see London or Paris or Hershey, Pennsylvania! I'll be poor and my husband will be a garage mechanic or a plumber's assistant or deliver kerosene, and I'll plant window boxes of geraniums and we'll end up sitting on a porch and I'll be a zombie, too! I'll never escape Travis! I just know it! Never!"

Jennifer suddenly burst completely into tears. I sat bolt upright on my branch. I put my arm around her. I didn't know what to say.

"You'll escape," I finally said softly.

"No, I won't."

"Yes, you will."

"No," she insisted. *"You'll* escape."

"What makes you think I won't end up a zombie, too?"

"You've already been out of this town. You're not like the other boys around here. I can see you're not *cursed*."

"Don't you have friends?"

"All the girls I know in this town are zombies-in-training. And all the boys can't wait to make them pregnant so they have to get married and go work at a factory, and end up as male zombies themselves. The biggest thrill any man in the history of Travis has ever had is buying a used Chevrolet. That's the highlight of their lives, and then it's downhill all the way. This town is a prison. It's death, with an annex in New Jersey."

"But if you know that, then you can stop it all from happening."

"How?" she asked, desperately.

"We'll find out how together. We'll be the best friends we can be and we'll save each other."

"We'll really be *best* friends!"

"Yes. Come on!" I shouted.

I climbed down out of the tree, with Jennifer right behind me. I took a penknife from my pocket.

"What're you doing?"

I started carving into the bark of the huge trunk of the apple tree. The bark fell away easily from my blade, and I was able to inscribe large, thick, and clear letters. Jennifer smiled when she saw I had carved the word ESCAPE.

"Now, this is our tree. Our own private tree," I told her. "And whenever we see it, even just the top of it from a block or a mile away, we'll know it belongs to us! It will remind us that we'll *both* escape. We will. We'll escape!"

Suddenly there came the scream of wild animals, and the twins were back upon us.

"What can we jump from now?" one of them wanted to know.

"We jumped off the garage, every ledge of the toolshed, all the trees, the fence, the front porch, and two barrels," the other specified.

"Then it's time for the apple tree again," I suggested.

Their eyes lit up.

But this time Jennifer and I climbed up, too. It all just seemed so stupid and dumb that even Jennifer and I got in the mood. We started jumping out of the tree with them. Jump and climb! Jump and climb! We jumped from higher and higher! We *climbed* higher and higher. Jennifer and I joined right in, shrieking with the twins like three Tarzans and a Jane, until we had climbed so high we were all frightened to leap. We were so high we were near the top, and for a while all any of us saw was miles and miles of a grand adventure stretching out before us.

I looked northeast, toward Manhattan, and I thought of Nonno Frankie.

CHAPTER SEVEN

Nonno Frankie Wakes Up the Zombies!

The next Saturday, Nonno Frankie and Nonna Mamie arrived bright and early in a different dumpy pickup truck. Nonno Frankie had hired a coworker of his from the Oreo batter vat team at NBC to bring out the tools and materials he'd need to get the summer planting under way. They unloaded a winepress, boxes of tomato plants, seeds, weird collapsible metal cages, pitchfork, rake, shovel, 300-foot garden hose, eight bags of sheep manure, and lots of shopping bags containing the ingredients for another intense eating experience.

Once they had all the stuff on the curb in front of the house, Nonno Frankie's cookie colleague drove off, and the twins, Nonno Frankie, and the rest of us carried the stuff inside.

Nonno Frankie locked the winepress up in the sturdy, dry toolshed because, he whispered to me, he didn't want the twins fooling around with it when he wasn't there. The press was the size of half a large barrel, with a long, thick handle attached to a metal screwing gizmo. If either of the twins decided to test it out on the other, they could easily squash a hand or head or whatever part of their anatomy they felt like experimenting with.

After that, the twins and I dashed around the place checking everything else out. Nonna Mamie and Nonno Frankie had brought so many intriguing things that weekend, I didn't hear my mother complain once. She did keep one eye open to make certain Nonno Frankie wasn't digging up any of her side of the yard, but on the whole, she didn't act wacky at all. One thing she did keep saying was, "Oh, kids, I think we're going to have our own Lassie!" She had gotten the job on the

ASPCA rabies van and was meeting a lot of dogs and dog owners. One of the pooches had an owner who knew of an old lady who had gotten arthritis and couldn't handle her pet collie anymore, and my mother had offered to take the dog off her hands. It was complicated, but Mom was supposed to find out during the next week if she'd be getting the collie or not.

"The dog's name is Queenie, but she's supposed to look exactly like Lassie," Mom said. "I heard when you walk her down the street, everyone calls out and asks if it's the *real* Lassie!"

Anyway, all of Saturday I helped Nonno Frankie mulch and plant a garden.

"Got to turn over the earth," Nonno Frankie sang as he pushed his foot down on the pitchfork. "Every year, you turn the dirt over and over, and start again!" Every once in a while he'd have to yell at the twins, because they were mainly interested in playing with the water hose and throwing sheep manure at each other.

"Look at the rainbow, Nonno!" they called, sending a powerful stream of water straight up into the air. They were so hyperactively freaky, they let the water fall right back down on them.

"Nonna Mamie fed them too much goat's milk

when they were born." Nonno Frankie sighed.

Jennifer came over at noon. I introduced her to everybody. She and Nonno Frankie hit it off right away, especially because she wasn't afraid to get her hands dirty, and pitched in to help with the planting.

"Ho! Ho! Ho! What runs around a yard but doesn't move?" Nonno Frankie quizzed Jennifer.

"I don't know," she said.

"A fence!" Nonno Frankie howled. "A fence!"

Jennifer managed to convincingly howl, too, and he really appreciated that. I had warned her his jokes weren't very funny, but Nonno Frankie's laugh was infectious.

"Ho! Ho! Ho!" Nonno Frankie went on, this time pointing across the airport toward the Con Edison electric plant. "I knew a man who got a big bill from that electric company. He was really *shocked!*"

I mean, Nonno Frankie had something funny or nice and human and interesting to say about everything. Jennifer held up her end of the conversation, too. She told him Indians used to live on the land before the town was founded. She said a lot of folks had found arrowheads and broken pieces of white clay pottery and peace pipes.

Nonno Frankie Wakes Up the Zombies!

"That reminds me," Nonno Frankie said. "You know what a small laugh is in the Indian language?"

"No."

"A MINNEHAHA!" Nonno Frankie howled, and we howled with him.

By mid-afternoon all the tomato plants were in, as well as eight rows of corn, three rows of beets, two of radishes, four of lettuce, and five of some weird vegetable called escarole.

After lunch, Jennifer introduced us to Leon and Rose Appling, two teenagers from the *downstairs* black family next door. Leon was thirteen, and Rose was fifteen. They were very nice, but painfully polite and shy. To be truthful, they reminded me of myself, which made me like them right away. They just leaned against the iron mesh of their chicken coop, a spot that had the best view of Nonno Frankie and the activity going on in our backyard. They were no blood relation to the water-head baby, which Mrs. Lillah was rocking in its carriage in the sunshine, but they did own all the barnyard animals including a white hen they called Miss White. The reason we got to know Miss White by name was because she was the one chicken smart enough to know how to escape from the chicken coop at least once a day and strut around our yard.

"I'm sorry about Miss White," Leon apologized, trying to call the chicken back over the fence. "We try to plug up all the holes, but she always finds another one."

"That's fine. We like animals," I explained.

Leon was happy to hear that. He had a round, pleasant face and a gap-toothed smile, and he practically always kept his hands in the pockets of his worn blue overalls. His sister, Rose, had a big nervous smile and long, thin arms and legs. Whenever she walked or leaned or sat, her limbs took a few seconds more to halt their moving and twitching after the rest of her body. Of course, Nonno Frankie warmed them up with a few jokes, and before we knew it Rose and Leon were letting us pet their rabbits. Nonno Frankie also gave them some radish and beet seeds and offered to catch Miss White for them and return her to their yard.

"What do you get if you cross a vampire with a skunk?" Nonno Frankie called out, chasing Miss White. "Ho! Ho! Ho! *A dirty look from the vampire!*" Nonno Frankie squealed.

I mean, everybody was having a lot of fun. But then Nonno Frankie started the main festivity of the day. "Let's catch crabs and killies!"

"What are killies?" Jennifer and I asked.

"Little fish," Nonno Frankie explained.

Within minutes, Nonno Frankie had a whole expedition organized to march to the Arthur Kill. It turned out the collapsible metal cages were crab traps, and he had a box with two wire-screen cylinders that he told us were the killie traps. It looked like it was going to be a great adventure, so I went looking for my sister, who hadn't been around for a while. Finally, I found her lying across the bed in her upstairs room. She was crying.

"What's the matter?" I asked.

"I saw the water-head baby," Betty sobbed.

"Oh."

I tried to explain to her how going to catch killies with us might take her mind off the sight of the baby, but she said she just wanted to stay in her room and be alone awhile. That's how my sister always was. She could be strong and tough one minute, flicking her long blond hair like nothing in the world could bother her, but then she'd see something cruel and unexplainable once in a while and go cry someplace where no one could see her. I had long ago learned to respect her feelings.

"You want me to stay with you?" I asked.

"No," she said. "I just need to cry awhile."

"Nonna Mamie told me she's making chicken parmigiana, roast peppers, and linguini for us tonight," I told her. That cheered her up a little.

VAROOOOOMMMMM!

Because of the airplanes taking off and landing, we had to walk along the edge of the airport. Three planes took off over our heads as Nonno Frankie led me, Jennifer, and the twins on our first trip to the river. We carried the traps, but Nonno Frankie hauled a shopping bag of fish heads, which he'd brought all the way down from the Fulton Fish Market in Manhattan. The whole trek wasn't much more than a mile.

Jennifer knew the way to the river from many years of playing there with her brothers when they were kids. But Nonno Frankie knew the names of the flora and fauna better than anyone. On our hike he pointed out wild beach plums, possum tracks, poison ivy, pieces of granite, blue jays, cardinals, sparrows and sparrow nests, chicken hawks circling in the sky, a turtle (the twins wanted to take it home, but he said "no"), and a garter snake.

Closer to the kill, Jennifer pointed out a sandy inlet where she told us all the Travis kids went swimming, but it was Nonno Frankie who selected a spot right at the river's edge where he wanted us to put out the crab and killie traps. Among the important things Nonno Frankie taught us that day were:

1) how to tie a fish head to the bottom of a crab trap so crabs can't steal the bait;
2) that killies look just like sardines;
3) why killies can swim into a narrow hole in a killie trap but then can't find their way out;
4) how to put a fish head on a string with a sinker attached to it, throw the line ten feet out, let it sink to the bottom, and then actually feel a crab eating the fish head;
5) how to gingerly pull a crab line in;
6) how to keep the crabs and killies you catch nice and moist in a burlap bag;
7) a lot of incidental information, such as the fact that "A MAN, A PLAN, A CANAL—PANAMA" backward and forward spells the same thing.

We started to catch killies all over the place. Nonno Frankie told us he was voted the best killie catcher in his hometown in Sicily, and it was easy to see that had to be the truth. We would have caught a lot more of everything if Nonno Frankie hadn't had to keep stopping the twins from trying to build rafts and launch themselves out into the kill. Their attention span for everything that afternoon, except raft building, was very short. Nonno Frankie sat Nicky and Joey down at one point and gave them a big lecture on how many kids die each year because they try to build rafts and then float to their deaths down rivers and streams. He acted out what it was like to drown, and even dropped down on the ground to portray to them how horrible it was to breath in the water. When that didn't seem to work, Nonno Frankie told them the real danger of being out in this channel was that there were killer whales in the Kill Van Kull renowned for devouring young boys on rafts. He also told them there were monstrous whirlpools that could spring up and suck them down through the earth to China. The twins found that idea scary for a while, but eventually they started building another raft.

Somehow we all made it back alive with all the killies we could carry, but only four crabs.

"Where are all the crabs?" Connie and Nonna Mamie wanted to know.

"On their honeymoons," Nonno Frankie explained. "In September they'll all be back from their honeymoons, and we'll catch dozens of them."

Jennifer was invited for dinner, so there were nine of us seated around Connie's kitchen table. Mom mainly talked about the Lassie she might get. Betty looked recovered from seeing the water-head baby. Connie wore a turban with rhinestones in it and told us glamorous details about the job as hatcheck girl, which she had landed. The twins played a predining game of rolling on the linoleum floor. Nonna Mamie was checking the cheese melt on the luscious-looking pounded and fried chicken cutlets. Nonno Frankie announced he would prepare the appetizer—killies.

We watched Nonno Frankie rinse the killies, drain them, and then toss them in flour. In a flash they were sizzling in a deep frying pan of oil. In less than five minutes the entire appetizer was in front of us on the table: a mountain of breaded midget fish with their heads still on. Mom and Betty said they weren't going to be having any. The twins ran away from the table to swat flies. Connie and Nonna Mamie were busy with the main course. That left me and Jennifer to sample Nonno Frankie's special treat.

"Enjoy! Enjoy!" Nonno Frankie instructed proudly.

Jennifer looked at me. I didn't want to hurt Nonno Frankie's feelings, so I reached out a fork, put one of the three-inch fish on my plate, and began to dissect it.

"No, no!" Nonno Frankie cried out. "This is the way you eat killies!"

He reached out his hand to the platter, snatched up five or six of the treats in his hand, and tossed them into his mouth like french fries with eyeballs.

"You eat them heads and all!" Nonno Frankie said. "Enjoy, everybody! Enjoy!"

"It's a great Italian delicacy," Connie confirmed.

If it was good enough for Nonno Frankie, I decided, it was good enough for me, so I grabbed a handful and started munching. Then Jennifer took a handful, and she started munching.

"May I use your bathroom a moment?" my mother asked Connie.

"Of course," Connie said.

Mom stood up from the table and walked past the kitchen stove to the door at the far left front of the room. She smiled graciously and closed the door.

I seemed to be the only one who heard her gagging.

By the time dinner was over, we had long forgotten the killies and were all so stuffed we could barely move.

"Now we need some entertainment," Nonno Frankie said.

"There *is* no entertainment in Travis," Jennifer apologized. She told him about the zombies and how all they did day and night was sit on their porches.

"Then we'll just have to liven those zombies up." Nonno Frankie winked.

"How can we do that?" I asked.

"Watch," Nonno Frankie said.

He went through the kitchen garbage and pulled out the tin cans Nonna Mamie had emptied to make the meal. There were all sorts of cans. Tomato paste cans. Garbanzo bean cans. Peeled zucchini cans. Empty olive oil cans. Nonno Frankie shoved them all in a bag, grabbed a big ball of twine, and went out to the front porch. It ended up just being me, Jennifer, and the twins helping Nonno Frankie tie the cans into two bunches. Then we carried them a little way up Glen Street.

"Here," Nonno Frankie said, halting at a spot that had two telephone poles directly across the street from each other. He tied one end of the string to one set of the cans; then he went across the street and tied the other end of the string to the second bunch of cans. Jennifer and I crossed with him to watch his handiwork.

"I see what you mean," Nonno Frankie said, eyeing the lit porches of the houses on the street. The zombies were sitting out in full force, snoozing or staring across to Cemetery Hill.

Nonno Frankie loosely wedged one part of the string behind a splinter of the telephone pole and the other end of the string loosely on a splinter of the second telephone pole. That left the string stretched two feet high straight across the road.

"Now we just sit on our porch and wait for a car," Nonno Frankie said.

I knew there wasn't much traffic ever on Glen Street. However, time never went slowly with Nonno Frankie around. He taught us a song called "Isle of Capri," showed us how to find the Big Dipper and the North Star, and told us eight jokes, including one about a boy skeleton who didn't want to go to school because he didn't have the guts for it. Jennifer, me and the twins were laughing our heads off so much we forgot about the biggest trap we'd set for the day.

"A car! A car!" Jennifer finally cried out, happier than I'd ever seen her.

Sure enough, a car had turned off Victory Boulevard, and was coming fast up Glen Street. We ducked before the car reached the telephone poles with the string. My heart was beating like it was going to jump out of my chest. For a second there was no sound and I thought the string might have broken, but I could see Nonno Frankie was calm and experienced in these matters. Then:

CLANG! BANG! SCRATCH! BAM! CLINK!

The clatter of tin cans! Loud, cacophonous cans being dragged along the street! The peaceful summer night was alive with rattling, eardrum-splitting sounds! The zombies awoke! They were up on their feet! The tin cans dragging along behind the car screamed at them, "Live! Live, you zombies! Live! Nonno Frankie is here!"

CHAPTER EIGHT

School Should Be a Big Pot of Juicy Meatballs!

That first summer I should have suspected that Nonno Frankie was becoming my pigman, but I didn't know then what a pigman was. One of the things a pigman does is help you, but sometimes someone can be helping you and you don't notice it. They help you in a lot of little ways and then suddenly one day it all adds up and you're able to say to yourself, "*This* person is my pigman." I didn't know Nonno Frankie was my pigman until that September, when summer vacation was over and I had to go to school. I really hated the idea of being the only new kid in my class.

Besides, the end of that summer had seen a number of changes in our house. The significant events were:

1) My mother picked up *four* free Lassie-looking dogs from her job with the ASPCA. Any time any dog remotely resembling a collie was turned in at the animal shelter, or she heard a rumor of someone wanting to get rid of a collielike animal, Mother snatched it up and brought it home. The collies' names were Queenie, Prince, Lady, and Rin Tin Tin. Only Queenie and Prince were pedigreed collies. Rin Tin Tin looked like a German shepherd with collie fur. Lady was all white and looked like an albino midget wolf. Mother said Lady could be my very own dog, but deep down I knew she didn't mean it. She'd control the dogs just like she tried to control Betty and me and everything else. But I loved Lady instantly, even though she was already three years old and had neurotic-looking eyes.

2) Mom let the dogs run loose in the house most of the time, but she built a wire-fence pen

next to the garage for them to hang out during the day when they got too wild.

3) Connie began to date "Chops" Tarinksi, a nice
butcher who owned the store on Victory
Boulevard that always had hundreds of
sausages hanging in its front window. My
mom was not thrilled with this budding ro-
mance.

4) The twins made bows and arrows and ran
around for weeks trying to shoot each other in
the ears.

5) Nonno Frankie pressed over fifty crates of
grapes to make gallons of blood-red wine,
which he stored in the toolshed.

6) I began to lose some of my shyness and put on
a ghost show in Leon and Rose Appling's dark
chicken coop. I had the kids each brought in
blindfolded, made spooky sounds, and then
tickled their ears with feathers so they'd think
there were evil spirits flying around their
heads. The climax of the show was when I
told the victims they had to shake hands with
a real ghost. Then I'd put a stuffed rubber
glove that had been dipped in oil and cold
cream into their hands, and they'd flee the
chicken coop screaming.

7) Miss White started eating bread crumbs out of my hand.
8) We set tin can traps over 126 times.
9) We helped Nonno Frankie harvest tasty prize tomatoes, pumpkins, and other vegetables.
10) Jennifer and I sat in our apple tree at least once a day, eating its giant red apples and discussing philosophic and scientific questions, like why everyone doesn't just fly off the earth since it's flying through space at 18-1/2 miles per second. We also carved our names in the tree by cutting away the bark so it now read "ESCAPE! PAUL & JENNIFER!"

As the first day of school came closer, I got sick to my stomach and thought at any time I was going to engage in reverse peristalsis. My mother took Betty and me to the Salvation Army charity store to get our back-to-school outfits, which wasn't as pathetic as it sounds. Mother had been getting our clothes at junk shops for years, but with her gift of gab she made a good contact with a lady General at the Salvation Army store, and she'd call my mom whenever some good used clothes in our sizes had been donated. I didn't feel funny about wearing used clothes because my mother had very good taste and usually picked us out decent outfits. I looked like a wreck sometimes though because of climbing the apple tree or tripping in mud puddles.

One day in the apple tree Jennifer and I decided to tell each other about the best teachers we'd ever had in school, and the worst.

"The first wonderful teacher I remember was Miss Stillwell," I said, munching on an apple.

"What was so hot about her?" Jennifer asked.

"She was my fifth-grade teacher and she'd let me and a friend go to the rear blackboard and draw pastel pictures whenever we finished our work. In one term we drew Mount Vernon, London Bridge, the Eiffel Tower, and an anteater."

"My favorite teacher was in the sixth grade," Jennifer said. "Miss Midgely. She invited the whole class over to her house for a picnic one day."

Before we knew it, we were remembering all sorts of things about our past teachers. I remembered Miss Wilmont, a teacher at one of my schools who came to class one day with a baby chipmunk tucked in her blouse to keep it warm and let it hear a heartbeat. And once she praised me for having decorated my biology notebook with a drawing of a life-size, grinning skull.

"The only thing I ever got attention for," Jennifer complained, "was in the fourth grade, when I made a vase out of a pickle jar covered in plaster of paris and decorated it with shiny buttons."

"I remember one teacher who taught me the difference between having a dog and a cat for a pet," I said.

"What?"

"Well, this lab teacher, Mr. Soifer, said the best way was to think how each pet would treat you if you were suddenly shrunk to three inches high."

"What's the difference?"

"He said a cat would instantly grab you like a mouse and chew on you, but a dog would just look a little puzzled and ask, 'Hey, boss, what happened?'"

The worst thing Jennifer came up with about a teacher was that she worked hard during her free period one term for a Miss Erskine, but Miss Erskine gave her only half a service credit when all the other teachers were giving their student slaves at least two whole service credits. The worst thing I could remember about a teacher was a Latin teacher at one school who used to seat us all according to our test marks. The kid with the highest mark got the first seat in the first row, and she often referred to the last couple of rows as the "really stupid rows." I also went to one school that had a crazy principal who used to come rushing into our classrooms with a ruler to make sure our windows weren't open more than six inches from the bottom. He used to drive the kids *and* the teachers nuts.

But it wasn't the new teachers I'd be having in Travis that made me nauseous. School was a sane place to me compared to my loving, wacko mother and all the weird apartments we had moved in and out of. What *was* bothering me was thinking about all the kids Jennifer told me I'd be meeting and what some of their character flaws were. She had even pointed out several teenage freaks on the street or coming out of Ronkewitz's Candy Store, which was right next to the school. The following is a list of the ones she highlighted, and her comments about them:

A) MOOSE KAMINSKI = "A big boy who is nice-looking but likes to push kids down on the ground and sit on them. He probably has a golden heart and could be a good friend to somebody equally demented, but he always ends up doing rotten things so everybody will think he's a big shot."

B) TOMMY ROSINSKI = "A nice weakling boy the gang calls CBRH, which stands for Cry Baby Rooster Head."

C) LOUIE ONTECKSKI = "Fifteen years old, gets left back a lot, very mature for his age and lives just outside of town in a house that looks like a junk-car lot."

D) ROBERT MUKSKI = "Thirteen, still wets his pants."

E) FRANK DESISKI = "Grins like an idiot a lot, but not a bad boy. Four feet high. Nicknamed 'Little Frankfurter.'"

F) JOHN QUINN = "A nice Irish boy, clean-cut, normal decent parents who don't do the polka."

G) ROSEMARY WINSKI = "Town tramp."

H) HELEN YANKOWITZ = "Town weirdo."

I) DEANNA DEESE = "Town stuck-up beauty."

J) CHRISTOPHER SUSALUS, TONY PARA-MUS, and SOPHIE MALLUS = "Sweet Greek teenagers bused in from farms their families own. Their parents don't let them date anyone except Greeks, they can only marry Greeks, and they can only work at Greek roadside fruit and vegetable stands all summer."

K) BUDDY CRABBSKI = "Was dropped on his head as a baby. A fat boy, looks like a Macy's Thanksgiving Day Parade balloon."

L) LEON BRONSKI = "One of Moose Kaminski's henchmen. Leon's father beats him up a lot."

M) MIKE BRONSKI = "Leon's older brother. Gets beat up by his father when his father can't find Leon."

N) JEANETTE FILOPOWITZ = "Nice girl who lives on our block."

O) DENNY KRAVITZ = "Looks like he just escaped from a reformatory. Has a skull shaped like a cone."

P) ELLEN FIGLER = "Nice girl."

Q) DORIS LASKI = "Nice girl, face like a woodchuck."

Anyway, the Sunday before I was to start school, Nonno Frankie saw me stumbling around in our half of the backyard in a frightened stupor. He called me over to him.

"You start school tomorrow?" he asked.

"Yes."

"You don't look happy about it."

"I'm not."

"You don't do good in school?"

"I got good marks in all the other schools I went to."

"You get along with teachers?"

"Yes."

"Good." Nonno Frankie smiled. "School should be a happy place. It should be like a big bubbling pot of juicy meatballs! You should eat it all up and join the CP Club."

"What's the CP Club?"

"The Clean Plate Club. You must gobble up school."

"What if it tries to gobble me up?"

"You don't let it. You learn the important rules, and then nothing and nobody can hurt you," Nonno Frankie said, giving me one of his winks. "You will meet pretty girls at school."

"Maybe they won't be so pretty."

"When I went to school in Italy, a girl could have a face like a train wreck as long as she was blond. Ho! Ho! Ho!"

I laughed weakly. "Jennifer told me there are some nasty kids at this school."

Nonno Frankie smiled sympathetically. "You'll

read, learn, and get smart!"

My mouth had gone dry. "I want all the kids to like me," I finally managed to say.

Nonno Frankie looked at me seriously. "Only dead fish swim with the stream. You just worry about liking yourself, that's what you should worry about!" He put his hand on my shoulder, and we stood at the edge of his tomato patch. "See! All the tomatoes have been picked. They all grew up and have gone into our stomachs! That's the rule of tomatoes! Tomatoes have rules, and I'll tell you all the rules *you* need to know for school. Have all the experiences you can. Experience is wonderful! It teaches you how to recognize all your mistakes when you make them over and over again! Do you mind me giving you advice?"

"No," I said. "I need all the advice I can get!"

It seemed strange Nonno Frankie was the one taking the time to care about what I was feeling. I remember thinking that maybe this is what fathers are supposed to do. Maybe this is why fathers exist. *Good* fathers, not absentee fathers or spirited wacked-out mothers.

"Don't be discouraged by fat books," Nonno Frankie warned me. "In every fat book, there's a little thin book trying to get out! And don't put grease on your hair the night before you're going to have a big test."

"Why not?"

"Everything might slip your mind! Ho! Ho! Ho! Get it?"

"Yes, Nonno Frankie."

"I'll teach you every rule I know about going to school. When in doubt, a closed mouth gathers no feet! And never get into rock fights with kids who have ugly faces, because they have nothing to lose! And never, *never* play leapfrog with a unicorn!"

Now *that* little thought made me smile.

CHAPTER NINE

My First Fistfight

When I think now about what it was like for me when I was a teenager, I have to admit that deep inside, my greatest need was to find a meaning to my life. Without meaning I suppose most everybody might as well be dead. Jennifer, Betty, my mother, Connie. It seemed to me that everybody was doing a desperate kind of dance to feel she was worth something. Jennifer was afraid she'd be trapped in Travis and become a zombie. My sister was still so afraid the world was rotten that she pretended she didn't even want to be part of it. Mom was frantic to get loot. That's the only way I can understand how she tried to become rich by having collies make love. She had tried so many other schemes: 1) selling costume jewelry from door to door; 2) selling home cosmetics; 3) coloring black-and-white photos; 4) running a hamburger stand; 5) being a riveter in a Staten Island shipyard; and 6) tending bar.

Now that she had two pedigreed collies, she encouraged them to be romantic night and day. She'd put Queenie and Prince in our side room, give them great room service like it was a bridal suite, sing for them, dance for them, and pump "Let's Make Love" on the Pianola. She'd never mentioned anything to Betty or me about love and sex, but she taught those dogs everything. And she still had a cold fish-eye toward Connie's using eyebrow tweezers and wearing tight dresses to further entice Chops, her butcher boyfriend.

But Nonno Frankie seemed to already *have* a meaning to his life. He had some secret about life that I very much wanted to know; and whatever that secret was, I suspected it was something he had learned over many, many years like the fermenting of a fine wine. I was sure he once had been a bumbling teenager like myself, but he had probably been through the mill and learned the hard way. Yet I felt that *I* was bringing meaning to his life. I mean, I knew he loved his tomatoes, and deep-frying breaded killies, and squeezing grapes, and walking across a field of grass and watching a wide channel flow. I knew his heart was filled with many joys, but it was big enough to fit me in, too. I think he very much wanted to help me be brave about life, or at least hopeful. Maybe he wanted me to be part of a new meaning to *his* life, too, a meaning other than his family and sauteed eels. The twins were too young to know they needed him yet, but I knew he'd be there for them when they stopped being so wild. And Connie was more interested in Chops Tarinski than in him. Nonna Mamie was short as a dwarf but strong and solid as an ox, so she didn't need much from him. In his own jolly and simple way, I think, Nonno Frankie needed to share his secrets with me.

The first morning of school I should have known there would soon be trouble because there were three ominous headlines in the local newspaper:

1) Voodoo Curse Turns Scottish Woman into a Cow!
2) Peanut Butter and Jelly Great for Kids' Halloween Makeup!

3) Reading Comic Books Discovered to Be
   Major Factor in Teenage Suicides!

I went to school anyway.

Mom had registered Betty and me the week before, so we just had to report to our different
homerooms. On the plus side, the school was not
too big and not too small. It had had a fresh paint
job inside and out. And there was a lot of yard
around the whole building for lunch breaks and
things like that. It had a fence around it, but not
the kind of fence used at reformatories where they
have very high, electrified ones covered with rolls
of barbed wire. This school had a low fence with
lots of open gates. It was just enough to define the
boundaries of the place and yet let everybody
rush out into the street in case it caught on fire or
blew up.

I was in Jennifer's homeroom which meant we
had Miss Haines for our homeroom teacher.
When I first met Miss Haines, she frightened me
because she was very large and looked like a
prison matron in a big silk dress.

"So, you're the new boy," Miss Haines said to
me, her face lighting up with a wicked smile. She
was a very animated person, with a very high

feminine voice and a laugh like an ambulance siren. She insisted I stand up and introduce myself to the class. I thought I would die. That's the kind of teacher Miss Haines turned out to be. A little bit fun, a little bit dangerous, and at least once a week she'd make everybody do something in front of the class that would make them want to die.

All the characters Jennifer had warned me about were in our homeroom. The worst boys sat in the back as a group: Moose Kaminski, Leon and Mike Bronski, Denny "Conehead" Kravitz, and Little Frankfurter. CBRH and "Bobby who still wets his pants" sat in the front, and in the middle there were a lot of the nice boys and girls including Doris "Woodchuck" Laski.

The way our programs turned out, Jennifer and I had homeroom with Miss Haines, and first period we had her for mathematics. Also, we both had Mr. Milton for history, Mr. Lahr for art, and Miss Rock for science. In addition, in fourth period we had lunch, which was like a visit to the bowels of the earth. The cafeteria was in the cellar, and you had to get a tray, get on line, and pass by a lot of steam tables where ladies who looked like escaped electric-shock nurses gave you plates of weird-looking food. The hamburgers tasted like filets of kangaroo meat. The spaghetti looked like skinny white worms in red mud. The beef stew was so congealed, you had to smack it with a soup-spoon to get it to break up. But that whole first week I didn't feel like eating, so the cuisine didn't bother me that much. Besides, they had good fresh milk, tasty butter, and great vanilla ice cream cups, and the staff tried hard to please. Also, there was a nice "slow" old man named Pops who used to sweep up the cafeteria while all the kids ate. Moose Kaminski and the Bronskis always made fun of him by secretly taping signs like "I'M A HALF-WIT" to his back, and sometimes they'd sneak up behind him with an empty milk con-tainer and stamp on it so it'd explode. Pops would be so startled, he'd drop his broom, but then he'd laugh and lope off shaking his finger at them like the good-natured Hunchback of Notre Dame he was.

When trouble came to me, it didn't involve any-body I thought it would. It involved the nice, nor-mal, smart boy by the name of John Quinn. Life does that to us a lot. Just when we think some-thing awful's going to happen one way, it throws you a curve and the something awful happens another way. This happened on the first Friday, during gym period, when we were allowed to play games in the school yard. A boy by the name of Richard Cahill, who lived near an old linoleum factory, asked me if I'd like to play paddle ball with him, and I said, "Yes." Some of the kids played softball, some played warball, and there were a few other games where you could sign out equipment and do what you wanted. What I didn't know was that you were allowed to sign out the paddles for only fifteen minutes per period so more kids could get a chance to use them. I just didn't happen to know that little rule, and Richard Cahill didn't think to tell me about it. Richard was getting a drink from the water fountain when John Quinn came up to me and told me I had to give him my paddle.

"No," I said, being a little paranoid about being the new kid and thinking everyone was going to try to take advantage of me.

"Look, you *have* to give it to me," John Quinn insisted.

That was when I did something berserk. I was so wound up and frightened that I didn't think, and I struck out at him with my right fist. I had forgotten I was holding the paddle, and it smacked into his face, giving him an instant black eye. John was shocked. I was shocked. Richard Cahill came running back and he was shocked.

"What's going on here?" Mr. Trellis, the gym teacher, growled.

"He hit me with the paddle," John moaned, holding his eye. He was red as a beet, as Little Frankfurter, Conehead, Moose, and lots of the others gathered around.

"He tried to take the paddle away from me!" I complained.

"His time was up," John said.

Mr. Trellis set me wise to the rules as he took John over to a supply locker and pulled out a first-aid kit.

"I'm sorry," I said, over and over again.

Then the bell rang, and all John Quinn whispered to me was that he was going to get even. He didn't say it like a nasty rotten kid, just more like an all-American boy who knew he'd have to regain his dignity about having to walk around school with a black eye. Before the end of school, Jennifer came running up to me in the halls and told me John Quinn had announced to everyone he was going to exact revenge on me after school on Monday. That was the note of disaster my first week at school ended on, and I was terrified because I didn't know how to fight. I had never even been in a fight. What had happened was all an accident. It really was.

CHAPTER TEN

My Second Fistfight

When Nonno Frankie arrived on Saturday morning, he found me sitting in the apple tree alone.
Mom had told him it was O.K. to walk around the
whole yard now, as long as he didn't do any dig-
gings or mutilations other than weed-pulling on
her side. I was expecting him to notice right off
the bat that I was white with fear, but instead he
stood looking at the carvings Jennifer and I had
made in the trunk of the tree. I thought he was

just intensely curious about what "ESCAPE! PAUL & JENNIFER!" meant. Of course, the twins, being such copycats, had already added their names so the full carving away of the bark now read "ESCAPE! PAUL & JENNIFER! & NICKY & JOEY!" And the letters circled halfway around the tree.

"You're killing it," Nonno Frankie said sadly.

"What?" I jumped down to his side.

"The tree will die if you cut any more."

I thought he was kidding, because all we had done was carve off the outer pieces of bark. We hadn't carved deep into the tree, not into the *heart* of the tree. The tree was too important to us. It was the most crucial place to me and Jennifer, and the last thing we'd want to do was hurt it.

"The heart of a tree isn't deep inside of it. Its heart and blood are on the *outside*, just under the bark," Nonno Frankie explained. "That's the living part of a tree. If you carve in a circle all around the trunk, it's like slitting its throat. The water and juices and life of the tree can't move up from the roots!" I knew about the living layer of a tree, but I didn't know exposing it would kill the whole tree. I just never thought about it, or I figured trees patched themselves up.

"Now it can feed itself from only half its trunk,"

Nonno Frankie explained. "You must not cut any more."

"I won't," I promised. Then I felt worse than ever. Not only was I scheduled to get beat up by John Quinn after school on Monday, I was also a near tree-killer. Nonno Frankie finally looked closely at me.

"Your first week at school wasn't all juicy meatballs?" he asked.

That was all he had to say, and I spilled out each and every horrifying detail. Nonno Frankie let me babble on and on. He looked as if he understood exactly how I felt and wasn't going to call me stupid or demented or a big yellow coward. When I didn't have another word left in me, I just shut up and stared down at the ground.

"Stab nail at ill Italian bats!" Nonno Frankie finally said.

"What?"

He repeated the weird sentence and asked me what was special about it. I guessed, "It reads the same backward as forward?"

"Right! Ho! Ho! Ho! See, you learn! You remember things I teach you. So today I will teach you how to fight, and you will smack this John Quinn around like floured pizza dough."

"But I can't fight."

"I'll show you Sicilian combat tactics."

"Like what?"

"Everything about Italian fighting. It has to do with your mind and body. Things you have to know so you don't have to be afraid of bullies. Street smarts my father taught me. Like 'Never miss a good chance to shut up!'"

VAROOOOOOOOOOM!

A plane took off over our heads. We walked out beyond the yard to the great field overlooking the airport.

Nonno Frankie suddenly let out a yell *"Aaeeeeeyaaaayeeeeeh!"* It was so bloodcurdlingly weird, I decided to wait until he felt like explaining it.

"Aaeeeeeyaaaayeeeeeh!" he bellowed again. "It's good to be able to yell like Tarzan!" he said. "This confuses your enemy, and you can also yell it if you have to retreat. You run away roaring and everyone thinks you at least have guts! It confuses everybody!"

"Is that all I need to know?" I asked, now more afraid than ever of facing John Quinn in front of all the kids.

"No. Tonight I will cut your hair."

"Cut it?"

"Yes. It's too long!"

"It is?"

"Ah," Nonno Frankie said, "you'd be surprised how many kids lose fights because of their hair. Alexander the Great always ordered his entire army to shave their heads. Long hair makes it easy for an enemy to grab it and cut off your head."

"John Quinn just wants to beat me up!"

"You can never be too sure. This boy might have the spirit of Genghis Khan!"

"Who was Genghis Khan?"

"Who? He once killed two million enemies in one hour. Some of them he killed with yo-yos."

"Yo-yos?"

"See, these are the things you need to know. The yo-yo was first invented as a weapon. Of course, they were as heavy as steel pipes and had long rope cords, but they were still yo-yos!"

"I didn't know that," I admitted.

"That's why I'm telling you. You should always ask about the rules when you go to a new place."

"I didn't think there'd be a time limit on hand-ball paddles."

"That's why you must ask."

"I can't ask everything," I complained.

"Then you *read*. You need to know all the rules wherever you go. Did you know it's illegal to hunt camels in Arizona?"

"No."

"See? These are little facts you pick up from books and teachers and parents as you grow older. Some facts and rules come in handy, some don't. You've got to be observant. Did you know that Mickey Mouse has only *four* fingers on each hand?"

"No."

"All you have to do is look. And rules change! You've got to remember that. In ancient Rome, my ancestors worshipped a god who ruled over mildew. Nobody does anymore, but it's an interesting thing to know. You have to be connected to the past and present and future. At NBC, when they put in a new cookie-cutting machine, I had to have an open mind. I had to prepare and draw upon everything I knew so that I didn't get hurt."

Nonno Frankie must have seen my mouth was open so wide a baseball could have flown into my throat and choked me to death. He stopped at the highest point in the rise of land above the airport. "I can see you want some meat and potatoes. You want to know exactly how to beat this vicious John Quinn."

"He's not vicious."

"Make believe he is. It'll give you more energy for the fight. When he comes at you, don't underestimate the power of negative thinking! You must have only positive thoughts in your heart that you're going to cripple this monster. Stick a piece of garlic in your pocket for good luck. A woman my mother knew in Palermo did this, and she was able to fight off a dozen three-foot-tall muscular Greeks who landed and tried to eat her. You think this is not true, but half her town saw it. The Greeks all had rough skin and wore backpacks and one-piece clothes. You have to go with what you feel in your heart. One of my teachers in Sicily believed the Portugese man-of-war jellyfish originally came from England. He felt that in his heart, and he eventually proved it. He later went on to be awarded a government grant to study tourist swooning sickness in Florence."

"But how do I hold my hands to fight? How do I hold my fists?" I wanted to know.

"Like *this!*" Nonno Frankie demonstrated, taking a boxing stance with his left foot and fist forward.

"And then I just swing my right fist forward as hard as I can?"

"No. First you curse him."

"*Curse* him?"

"Yes, you curse this John Quinn. You tell him, 'May your left ear wither and fall into your right pocket!' And you tell him he looks like a fugitive from a brain gang! And tell him he has a face like a mattress! And that an espresso coffee cup would fit on his head like a sombrero! And then you just give him the big Sicilian surprise!"

"What?"

"You *kick* him in the shins!"

※

By the time Monday morning came, I was a nervous wreck. Nonno Frankie had gone back to New York the night before, but had left me a special bowl of pasta and steamed octopus that he said I should eat for breakfast so I'd have "gusto" for combat. I had asked him not to discuss my upcoming bout with my mother or sister, and Betty didn't say anything so I assumed she hadn't heard about it.

Jennifer had offered to get one of her older brothers to protect me, and, if I wanted, she was willing to tell Miss Haines so she could stop anything from happening. I told her, "No." I thought there was a chance John Quinn would have even forgotten the whole incident and wouldn't make good on his revenge threat. Nevertheless, my mind was numb with fear all day at school. In every class I went to, it seemed there were a dozen different kids coming over to me and telling me they heard John Quinn was going to beat me up after school.

At 3 P.M. sharp, the bell rang.

All the kids started to leave school.

I dawdled.

I cleaned my desk and took time packing up my books. Jennifer was at my side as we left the main exit of the building. There, across the street in a field behind Ronkewitz's Candy Store, was a crowd of about 300 kids standing around like a big, undulating horseshoe, with John Quinn standing at the center bend glaring at me.

"You could *run*," Jennifer suggested, tossing her hair all to the left side of her face. She looked much more than pretty now. She looked loyal to the bone.

"No," I said. I just walked forward toward my fate, with the blood in my temples pounding so hard I thought I was going to pass out. Moose and Leon and Mike and Conehead and Little Frankfurter were sprinkled out in front of me like ushers from Hell, goading me forward. I didn't even hear what they said. I saw only their faces distorted in ecstasy and expectation. They looked like the mob I had seen in a sixteenth-century etching where folks in London had bought tickets to watch bull-dogs attack a water buffalo.

John stood with his black eye, and his fists up.

I stopped a few feet from him and put my fists up. A lot of kids in the crowd started to shout, "Kill him, Johnny!" but I may have imagined that part.

John came closer. He started to dance on his feet like all father-trained fighters do. I danced, too, as best I could. The crowd began to scream for blood. Jennifer kept shouting, "Hey, there's no need to fight! You don't have to fight, guys!"

But John came in for the kill. He was close enough now so any punch he threw could hit me. All I thought of was Nonno Frankie, but I couldn't remember half of what he told me and I didn't think any of it would work anyway.

"*Aaeeeeeyaaaayeeeeeeh!*" I suddenly screamed at John. He stopped in his tracks and the crowd froze in amazed silence. Instantly, I brought back my right foot, and shot it forward to kick John in his left shin. The crowd was shocked, and booed me with mass condemnation for my Sicilian fighting technique. I missed John's shin, and kicked vainly again. He threw a punch at me. It barely touched me, but I was so busy kicking, I tripped myself and fell down. The crowd cheered. I realized everyone including John thought his punch had floored me. I decided to go along with it. I groveled in the dirt for a few moments, and then stood up slowly holding my head as though I'd received a death blow. John put his fists down. He was satisfied justice had been done and his black eye had been avenged. He turned to leave, but Moose wasn't happy.

"Hey, ya didn't punch him enough," Moose complained to John.

"It's over," John said, like the decent kid he was.

"No, it's not," Moose yelled, and the crowd began to call for more blood. Now it was Moose coming toward me, and I figured I was dead meat. He came closer and closer. Jennifer shouted for him to stop and threatened to pull his eyeballs out, but he kept coming. And that was when something amazing happened. I was aware of a figure taller than me, running, charging. The figure had long blond hair, and it struck Moose from behind. I could see it was a girl and she had her hands right around Moose's neck, choking him. When she let him go, she threw him about ten feet, accidently tearing off a religious medal from around his neck. Everyone stopped dead in their tracks, and I could see my savior was my sister.

"If any of you tries to hurt my brother again, I'll rip your guts out," she announced.

Moose was not happy. Conehead and Little Frankfurter were not happy. But the crowd broke up fast and everyone headed home. I guess that was the first day everybody learned that if nothing else, the Zindel kids stick together. As for Nonno Frankie's Sicilian fighting technique, I came to realize he was ahead of his time. In fact, these days it's called karate.

CHAPTER ELEVEN

My Mother Kills Lady, and My Sister's Eyeballs Roll Backward up into Her Head!

The morning after the fight, the principal, Mr. Davis, sent for me and John Quinn to come to his office. He made us shake hands, and John and I became friends. We only tried to punch each other one other time, but that was more for fun.

You know, when you look back on the past and try to remember what it was like to be a teenager, you can't remember every single detail. Most of what I remember has to do with Nonno Frankie. Of course, a lot of the past doesn't mean anything,

113

but there are highlights you remember, and those highlights sometimes are pieces of a big puzzle that come together in the end as sure as destiny.

The next few months, I didn't mind going to school at all, and I especially enjoyed playing warball in the gym. With the cold weather coming on, warball was the big indoor game, and I liked trying to sock Moose with the ball. He'd always be on the opposite team from me, and I'd try to smack him with the ball so he'd be out of the game. He liked to aim at me, too, but I was fast and usually faked him out. I relished hitting Conehead with the ball, too, because the shape of his skull would make the ball fly off in all sorts of unpredictable directions.

By December, Queenie had given birth to her first litter of nine puppies, so, including Prince, Lady, and Rin Tin Tin, we had thirteen dogs in the house. None of the puppies were selling even though my mother advertised in both the Bayonne, New Jersey, *Gazette* and the Staten Island *Advance*, but she fantasized they would go like hotcakes in the spring.

Now that we had so many collies, I began to actually believe Lady was my own personal dog like Mom had told me. Lady was a wild, albino, wolf-spirited dog to begin with, and I played games with her that made her even wilder. We had a lot of fun romping together. But then something awful happened. Mom had gotten my sister a new frilly used hat from the Salvation Army store, and Betty liked it so much, she put it on and came running to the top of the steps calling out and imitating Scarlet O'Hara's voice. Lady and I were downstairs; we came out of the side room, where I had been cleaning up after the puppies and pumping "Hungarian Rhapsody" on the Pianola. Lady looked up with her neurotic eyeballs, didn't recognize Betty, ran up, and bit her. It wasn't a big bite, and when Betty cried out in surprise, Lady realized who it was and felt terrible. Lady began to whine and lick Betty's hand for forgiveness. That evening, though, Mom had a veterinarian come and give Lady a shot that she said was going to put Lady to sleep. Whenever Mom got rid of any pets we had, she never said she was killing them; she was just "putting them to sleep."

The next morning, Mom had Betty and me lift up Lady by her legs and bring her out to bury her in the backyard. Lady was stiff as a board, and I cried, but we managed to make a decent grave for her not far from the apple tree. The ground was hard and cold, and it took a lot of work with a shovel and pitchfork. It was good I had learned a long time before not to really and fully trust my feelings about anything where Mom was concerned. The rest of the day Betty and I spent finding stones to put on top of Lady's grave so possums and raccoons wouldn't dig her up.

After Lady died, my sister caught a very bad case of the flu and ran a high temperature. I don't think one thing had anything to do with the other, but I knew Betty hid her emotions even deeper than I did. She was older than me, so that made her the first line of defense against any emotional outbursts Mom might make regarding anything. One night, my sister's temperature got to be way over 100 degrees Fahrenheit, and even Mom got worried. She made me sit at the bottom of Betty's bed to watch her while she went down to ask Connie if she had any cold orange juice. She wasn't gone more than a minute when Betty sat upright against her pillows and looked at me strangely. I knew something terrible was going to happen.

"What's the matter?" I asked.

Betty stared at me and began to shake. Suddenly, her eyes fluttered. Then her eyelids froze open and her eyeballs rolled backward up into her head. Where her eyes had been, there were now nothing but two big white marbles.

"What's happening, Betty? What's happening?" I yelled, reaching out to touch her, to let her know I was there. Then her entire body went into a pulsing convulsion.

"She's going! She's going!" I shouted for Mom. I don't know why I picked those particular words. "Mom! She's *going!*"

Mother rushed upstairs and saw Betty in the middle of the fit.

"Get ice!" Mom screamed at me. "Ice!"

I got the ice cubes from the upstairs and downstairs refrigerators, then ran around the neighborhood collecting ice from Jennifer and people I didn't even know. We made an ice bath for Betty, and her fever finally came down. She was fine in a couple of weeks, charging off to school as strong as ever.

Moose Kaminski used to always say my sister was stuck-up and walked like she was bent backward over a barrel. He'd say I walked like I was bent forward over a barrel. I once told him he walked like he was bent *inside* a barrel, which he didn't like, so he wrestled me down to the ground and sat on me. Like I said, he sat on almost all the kids from time to time, so I didn't take it personally. Usually, he'd just rub a little dirt on me and say a couple of nasty things. Then he'd get up and go on his way. Most of the kids in Travis knew that Life had bigger kids in it, and sometimes they sat on you. That's just the way Life was. What I didn't know was that Moose was going to turn into a killer, but I'll get to that part later.

Most of my teenage life I didn't know what I was doing, but Nonno Frankie helped me whenever I asked, or if he noticed something was bothering me. A pigman notices things like that.

For example, Jennifer and I both didn't know how to catch a baseball. Neither of us had any serious training with anything smaller than a basketball. I never even *saw* my father during these years, let alone played catch with him. Whenever my gym class went to Schmul Park near the school for a real game of softball, no team would really want me, so I'd be picked last. I'd always be put out in left field, and whenever a ball came my way, I'd try my hardest to get under it and catch it. Most times the ball would go between my hands and hit me on the chest or head.

When Nonno Frankie found out about this, he

began playing catch with me, Jennifer, and the twins every weekend.

"Keep your eye on the ball!" he'd constantly shout. "Keep your eye on the ball!"

Thanks to Nonno Frankie we all improved at catching, but some balls would still bounce off my skull. And I wasn't good at football, particularly since Moose liked to grab the ball, run, and straight-arm me in the face. Nonno Frankie told me it wasn't important if I didn't have a great talent to play football because he thought the game was a case of twenty-two humans badly overexercising on a field, being watched by thousands of sitting humans badly in need of exercise.

What Jennifer and I *were* good at was sled riding down Cemetery Hill. Right from the first snowfall that winter, it was clear we were the perfect team to get the greatest speed and distance coming down the slopes, and we hit the fewest tombstones. Conehead and Little Frankfurter looked the most jealous about the kind of distance we could manage, even with a good "bump and jump" here and there. Moose just glared meanly at anything we did.

That winter, as the puppies grew bigger, they ate more and more food. Also, the car froze up with everything else during January and February. The snowfall was so heavy during those months that many times the buses didn't run and there was no way for Connie or Mom to get to work. Mother finally got laid off from her job anyway because the ASPCA free pet vaccination program was suspended. It'd start up again in the summer, but that was a long ways off. And for three weekends in a row Nonno Frankie and Nonna Mamie couldn't even make it down from Manhattan because the ferryboats ran into ice floes; and even if a boat was running, the #112 bus to Travis wasn't.

Dry dog food wasn't very expensive, but one day we were really low on human food. That day, Miss White, the chicken from the Appling family next door, made the mistake of getting out of her coop, the way she usually did, and was strutting around trespassing in our backyard. We had nothing for Sunday dinner except a few strands of old spaghetti, and there was no expectation of any meat for the next week because Connie had had a lovers' quarrel with Chops Tarinski. Although Connie liked to dress and make herself up glamorously, she had been raised on a farm, and one of her country talents came in handy that day. She and Mom gave the twins some crumbs of bread, which they took outside to sprinkle a trail so it led right into the back door of the house. Miss White pecked at the tasty crumbs, clearly thinking them quite a find in the snow, and eventually she just pecked her way right inside. Connie was hiding behind the door, slammed it shut, scaring the dickens out of Miss White, then grabbed her and broke her neck. It was quick and painless, though Betty and I didn't find out about this until we came down to dinner and found a scrawny-looking roast chicken sitting on a platter in the middle of the table. We asked where it came from because we knew we didn't have any money. The twins started to tell us, but Mom and Connie said "Shhhhh!" to them and gave them a dirty look.

I suspected the worst.

"Is . . . is that Miss White?" I stuttered.

"Yes!" the twins cried out with pride.

Betty and I got up from the table and went up-stairs. We searched our kitchen cabinets and fi-nally found a can of tuna fish. We dined on it in silence.

The next day Mom decided to overcome her deep man-hating tendencies and told Connie she should patch things up with Chops Tarinski. Con-nie was thrilled when Mom said it would be O.K.

to let him come visit her at the house, which is what the fight had been about in the first place. Chops couldn't understand why Connie wasn't allowed to have him in her own apartment. Apparently, he had told her he adored her, and wanted to start feeling more like part of her family. Connie told us he really wanted to get to know Nicky and Joey better, which didn't look like it sat very well with Mom for some reason. Anyway, Chops was invited to come over, but Mom told Connie to suggest to him that instead of candy or flowers, hamburger meat and rib-eye steaks would be more cherished. However, Mom also gave strict instructions to Connie that she couldn't "make out" with Chops under our roof, that it was not a suitable activity in a house filled with innocent youth.

I didn't think any more about the matter until one night I woke up to strange sounds coming from downstairs. I looked at the clock and saw it was past two A.M., and the first thought that passed through my mind was that a maniac was trying to break into the house to cut our throats. Of course, it would *take* a maniac to try to break into our house, which had over a dozen dogs. My next thought was that the strange bumping sounds I heard were from aliens trying to signal me in

Morse code that I was too good for this world and should return with them to their planet. The more awake I became, the more realistic I was, and I decided to creep down the stairs toward the sounds. I tiptoed because I didn't want the puppies in the side room to think it was feeding time and have them go berserk waking up the whole house.

Halfway down the stairs, I was sorry I had started. The front hallway was truly dark and shadowy now, and I felt very, very alone. The eerie bumping sounds continued, and I wanted to run back to bed, but I was drawn further and further down the stairs as if Druids had mesmerized me. The draft near the front door was especially chilling, as if many ghouls were floating all about me. I turned and started down the hall past the cryptlike slab of wall. The sounds were coming from the direction of the small dark storeroom straight ahead. More than ever the doorway looked like a huge beast's mouth. The door to Connie's bedroom was closed, but a slit of light glowed from the crack in the bathroom door. The crack looked even more like it had been made by an ax murderer, and the coldness of the room reminded me of my first fears about it. This was a room where something awful would happen, perhaps *was happening!*

The sounds came from the bathroom. I put my eye to the crack. At first, I could see only the other bathroom door. It was closed and its hook locked in place. The crack was too narrow to see the whole room, but by stretching my right eyeball far to the right, I saw a man had a woman up against the wall. At first it looked like he was strangling her, or had his teeth sunk deep into her neck like a vampire. The bumping sound turned out to be the woman's elbows and head gently hitting the plumbing pipes as the man pressed against her. All it turned out to be was Chops Tarinski kissing Connie Vivona.

"Hey, Mom!" I heard the twins calling from the other side of the door. "Mom, what are you *doing?*"

"Nothing, darlings," Connie called back. "Go back to sleep."

I tiptoed back out of the storeroom, but I still couldn't shake the feeling that someday something would happen there. Something terrible one day *soon*.

CHAPTER TWELVE

God, Death, and Boiling Lobsters

By the time spring came around, there had been a lot of death and destruction. It depressed me and Jennifer. We started having regular discussions about death while sitting up in our apple tree. Besides the deaths of Lady and Miss White, there were a number of other events that weighed us down:

1) The water-head baby had died at Easter, which everyone had expected anyway, but it

was sad to see Mrs. Lillah sitting out in front of her house with no baby carriage to rock.

2) Jennifer and I tried to transplant fish we caught from Willowbrook Lake to a small pond behind my house, but they only lived two days before turning belly-up, probably because the pond didn't have enough plants and oxygen to support them. The fish had been handsome pike, each over a foot long, strong, healthy fighting fish with iridescent backs and sharp teeth. But we had doomed them by wanting to keep them in our own private puddle.

3) Next, we thought we could at least make a beautiful terrarium in the backyard. All we did was dig a hole two feet wide, four feet long, and one foot deep, and plant in it some of the most healthy and appealing clumps of grass, Johnny-jump-up flowers, and other succulent flora. We then decided to add insects to it such as black beetles, ants, grasshoppers, centipedes, daddy longlegs, wood bugs, and cocoons. We designed everything perfectly. The terrarium became our lovingly controlled little universe where nothing could go wrong. We watered it. Replenished it. We did every-

thing except sufficiently wonder one day why Moose and the Bronski boys were watching us so long from across Victory Boulevard. We would see them passing by from time to time as we were digging and planting, but we didn't think they'd do what they did. What happened was, one morning Jennifer came over to play a board game with me called Rich Uncle, and afterward we strolled out to visit our perfect plant-and-insect world. We gasped at what we saw. Somebody, and we knew who, had smashed it with rocks and thrown dirt in it. Jennifer trembled, her voice cracking. "They've killed our little world," she said, stunned. I put my arm around her. We felt awful, but there was nothing we could legally do about it. We couldn't call the police and press charges against Moose and the Bronskis for annihilating a hole-in-the-ground terrarium.

And Miss Haines had done her share to depress us. She embarrassed me and everybody else one day by announcing her homeroom students' Intelligence Quotient Test results.

Miss Haines prefaced her remarks with "You'll never guess who got the highest score. Someone none of us thought was really smart!"

That someone turned out to be *me*, which didn't make me any extra friends. Miss Haines announced Jennifer's score, which was a normal I.Q. Moose turned out to have the intelligence quotient of a turtle. It was all just mortifying to everyone, but Miss Haines licked her chops as she announced each score. Jennifer's eyes filled up with tears at just having to witness the ordeal. Actually, her eyes filled with tears whenever we spoke about anything that might negatively influence her future, because she truly believed she had no future. She acted as though her spirit still felt condemned to her becoming a zombie, though I always tried my best to let her know she could be anything she wanted. I wasn't much comfort, though, because she knew I was completely mixed up myself. I had no idea how I would ever grow up to earn money to support myself, even though I liked science and math.

However, my favorite teacher in Travis turned out to be my English teacher, Miss Konlan. She was the only one besides Jennifer and Nonno Frankie who, I was positive, didn't think I was a misfit. She was the first high school teacher I had ever heard of who had a doctorate in Shakespearean studies. She was so brilliant, I was one of the few kids in her classes who wasn't bored and didn't throw pennies or shoot spitballs at her. She loved to hear about my ghost shows and encouraged me to write all sorts of weird tales and build 3-D cycloramas. But in April she had a severe nervous breakdown and they took her away. I was there in her class the day she broke down. I saw it! She was reading a beautiful speech from *Romeo and Juliet* when Moose, Conehead, and the Bronskis began launching paper airplanes and shooting kidney beans at her. The missiles would bounce off her head, *Boi-n-n-g! Boi-n-n-g!*, until she couldn't stand it any longer. Suddenly, she opened the classroom window wide and leaped up on the windowsill. It was three stories high above a cement handball court! And she pleaded desperately with the class: "If you don't stop it, I'm going to jump!" And that was the first time I learned how much most kids like action and suspense, because half the class yelled, "JUMP!"

I didn't just sit there.

I stood up and yelled at the worst hoods, telling them what a pack of barbarians they were. I knew my little speech wasn't going to make me any more popular, but it gave enough time for Mr.

Nash, the Dean of Boys, to run into the room and pull Miss Konlan off the windowsill. I began to think it was something about me that made people want to commit suicide. The month before, my mother had gotten feeling so down about the puppies' not selling, she threatened to kill herself by swallowing a pound of salt. Of course, my mother's threats weren't very real, but to have my sensitive, lovely English teacher driven to climb onto a window ledge was very upsetting. Naturally, we were told she wasn't coming back, so they gave us a substitute, Mr. Wender, who had all the sensitivity of a tsetse fly and killed off any spirit of creativity anyone had.

I really missed Miss Konlan. I wrote the best stories I ever did for her. One was about a man who ran a grocery store and would mix up a ton of wheat, corn, and beans every night and then tell his stepson that if he didn't have them separated by the morning, he would cut off his ears. But I had a sorcerer appear and bring an army of magical Japanese beetles to help him sort out the grains. And in another story I had a witch threaten to make a handicapped girl marry someone she didn't love if she didn't collect an armful of wool

from a flesh-eating llama, but an old man appeared
and taught her how to gather the wool from the
thorned branches of a thicket where the monster
llama had grazed. Miss Konlan would let me tell
her all my stories. She'd sit there smiling at me,
encouraging me. I even read to her an essay I
wrote in which I invented the perfect sleeping
room: a room that's painted all black with just a
mattress, where a boy could have fantastic dreams
of Heaven and Earth! She let me tell her my worst
fears about being a freak, and a social failure, and
a teenager who didn't know what on earth would
happen to him. But she said she was certain I had
nothing to worry about, that I was filled with life!
Filled! That I had magic! There was magic in me
to protect me from demons! That I'd always find a
way out! I'd escape! I'd be a winner!

During May, Jennifer and I continued to spend a
lot of time talking about death. Even on weekends
we'd sit in our apple tree lamenting the existence
of the Grim Reaper. The tree was in full blossom.
Its perfume filled the air. The weather was pleasant, so the zombies began to sit out on their
porches again. And Nonno Frankie began to plant
his new garden. One day, he came over to us in

the apple tree and did his best to cheer us up.

"What kind of apple has a short temper?" he asked.

"A crab apple," Jennifer sighed.

"Right! Ho! Ho! Ho! But do you know what game can be dangerous to your mental health?"

"Marbles, if you *lose* them," I answered, trying to force a smile.

"Here's one I'll bet you don't know," Nonno Frankie said, desperate to entertain us. "What do you get if you cross a pet dog and a werewolf?"

"What?" we asked to humor him.

"A new owner every full moon! Ho! Ho! Ho!"

We could hardly hear him because Queenie had had another litter of puppies, so now there were twenty-six collies in the outside pen. They were just barking and barking for no special reason. Mother had gone out to answer an ad to be a practical nurse, and Connie was out joyriding with Chops in his Buick Skylark. The twins were off to play at Schmul Park.

Nonno Frankie's worn blue work shirt and brown corduroy pants billowed in the wind, and his eyes shone like those of an earnest clown. At one point he made believe he needed our help putting in tomato plants, which he really didn't.

Finally, he could stand it no longer and just flat-out asked, "What's the matter with you two?"

"We don't want to die," I summarized.

"What do you mean, you don't want to die?"

"We don't *ever* want to die," Jennifer clarified, as we climbed down from our favorite branch. Of course, Nonno Frankie noticed Jennifer already had tears in her eyes. He watched us sink into a sitting position with our backs against the trunk right beneath where "ESCAPE! PAUL & JENNIFER! & NICKY & JOEY!" was carved. Nonno Frankie sat down, too, so now there were three of us sitting under the apple tree. He let us pour out our terrible feelings to him about the demise of Lady and the dead water-head baby and Miss Konlan trying to jump out the window. And our poor fish. There was death all around us, including the remnants of the destroyed terrarium, which looked like a little freshly dug grave.

"Death is the Great Mystery of life," Nonno Frankie said. This time, there was no Ho! Ho! Ho! in his eyes or voice at all. "But you're both too young to worry about it. You should only *wonder* about it, wonder about all the great questions such as 'Which came first, the chicken or the egg?'"

"Which did?" Jennifer wanted to know.

"Personally, I think the chicken," Nonno Frankie said.

"Why?" we asked.

"Because I can't see God wanting to sit around on an egg for over twenty days to hatch it," Nonno Frankie explained over the din of the collies yapping from their pen. "And you've got to remember most people only croak when they're very sick or very old, and you two kids aren't either of those. You shouldn't waste your days thinking a meteor's going to strike you and turn you into pancakes."

"We try to think about other things," I said. "But we always come back to death."

"Yesterday, we tried thinking about the universe," Jennifer added.

"The universe!" Nonno Frankie erupted. "How can you know the secrets of the universe when you can't even make a good tomato sauce yet! First things first. Besides, I think Death is nothing more than Nature's way of helping us say we've had enough baked ziti."

"We heard human beings' hair and fingernails continue to grow for three days after they die," I said.

"Sure," Nonno Frankie admitted, "but homework

stops immediately. See, you've got to always think of the big pluses! And one of the best ways to have people say nice things about you is to kick the bucket."

Jennifer started to weep. "Life is so painful," she said.

I could see Nonno Frankie wanted to give her a grandfatherly hug. For a long while the three of us just sat in silence, as the collies barked louder and louder.

"Do you think a dead person feels it when they're cremated?" I asked.

"No," Nonno Frankie said. "It's only the living things you have to worry about. Like lobsters. They feel pain when they're boiled alive, which is why you should always give them a good soak in a pot of salt water first. It numbs them."

Jennifer sobbed audibly. "God is so cruel."

"No," Nonno Frankie contradicted. "God is very kind. He's pulled strings so most of us can live a very long time. Even if we're starving, he's arranged it so we can live by eating our shoes."

"Eating our shoes?" I asked.

"Yes. He's made us so talented, we can live from eating shoe leather! A lot of people don't know that about God. And I'm not saying I'm personally thrilled about death. When I was your age, I sat around for a week and thought about it, but that was all."

"Only a week?" Jennifer inquired.

"Yes. I thought everything I could about death. I had read in one of my uncles' books about a Mongolian ruler who used to build pyramids out of human and camel skulls. And I worried about the body of Voltaire, who my teachers told me was a very famous person but whose body was stolen from its tomb and never found. I thought about a lot of things that one week. Things that bothered me even more than death. I didn't like finding out that Julius Caesar was an epileptic. I didn't like reading in an Italian history book that Christopher Columbus had blond hair. I hated learning anything that wasn't the way I wanted it to be. Old men in my hometown thought they could learn answers from God by placing a rooster down in a circle and watching which way it turned. My mama in Sicily believed God sent omens to her in the first words she would hear after waking up. Once, the first thing she heard was my papa ask for a coffee and proscuitto ham sandwich. She sat around all morning wondering what God was trying to tell her. And I had an aunt in Padua who thought divine revelation came through 'reading' the location of moles on her children's bodies. But more than anything, what really terrified me the one week I spent thinking about death was when I read what the last words of Michelangelo were!"

"What were they?" Jennifer and I both wanted to know.

"They were 'I don't feel so good,'" Nonno Frankie said. "That really scared me."

The collies now yapped at the top of their lungs, though it wasn't anywhere near feeding time. Mom had given everyone strict rules that when she wasn't home, all the dogs had to be kept only in the side room or in their pen, so I figured it was better for them to be outside in the fresh air.

I caught Nonno Frankie looking to the dogs, and then glancing up toward the window from which my mother had yelled at him about keeping off her half of the backyard. He seemed to be making some connection between the dogs, my mother, and me. The way he had been talking, the way he was looking at me, this was the moment I realized he was much more than Ho! Ho! Ho!

"You only think about death when you are not alive. When you are not alive *inside*," Nonno Frankie said, pointing toward his heart. "It's hard to think of life when you are not allowed to be free and alive."

"How can we feel free and alive?" we asked.

"Don't let other people make you feel dead."

"But how?"

"Don't let the zombies and witches drag you down. Believe in yourself and in your own heart and mind, and don't go around thinking the veal cutlets are always tastier in another frying pan. You need to know you are your *own* frying pan. Shut out wacko mothers and rocking-chair mummies and anyone else who doesn't see how delicious you are inside! You are two wonderful kids! But you are trapped! The zombies and wackos have made you forget how buttery and sweet you are! You are a wonderful boy and girl! If one of your legs is shorter than the other, that is something you maybe can't change. But that has nothing to do with being good, bad, or worthless, or nice. You stop thinking about death when you start knowing who you really are. Each of you is one of a kind. You are like homemade salad dressings. No two come out the same. A little less vinegar there, a little more olive oil here. You are like fingerprints on a knife! Each is different! Each of you is the only one of you who will ever dance your own tarantella. And when you remember that, and remember to listen to yourself, then you don't think of Death anymore! You think of Life! Listen! Can't you hear all the Life?"

Jennifer and I listened.

What we heard was the collies barking their heads off.

Nonno Frankie stood up. He was alert, filled with energy, knowing what he was about to do. He started walking swiftly toward the dog pen. Jennifer and I leaped up and hurried to catch up with him.

"Do you know what 'Io sono differente!' means in Italian?" he asked.

"No," we said.

"It means 'I am different!'"

The dogs barked louder, jumping higher up against the fence the closer we got to them. In a moment, Nonno Frankie was at their gate. He released the latch and threw open the gate. Twenty-six collies came rushing out into the backyard. Big Lassies! Small Lassies! All sizes of Lassies jumping on us, kissing us, licking our faces. Nonno Frankie began to run toward the back fence. Jennifer and I and the dogs took off after him. In a moment we were all racing across the great fields above the airport. Young skunk cabbages and stalks of lady's slipper flowers and bullrushes and wild wheat were all reaching upward toward the dazzling new spring sun!

"IO SONO DIFFERENTE!" Nonno shouted at the sky.

"IO SONO DIFFERENTE!" Jennifer and I cried out. "IO SONO DIFFERENTE!"

We ran yelling proudly, victoriously, all of us leaving Death, we thought, far, far behind.

CHAPTER THIRTEEN

The Slaying of the Apple Tree

The fascinating thing to Jennifer and me was that, after the romp, all the dogs followed Nonno Frankie back to their pen like contented, well-adjusted canines. None of us want to run crazy all the time, but once in a while it does a living spirit good. From that day forward, Jennifer and I swore we would never forget the importance of freedom and being a little daring about life. We even started going up in airplanes. Of course, we didn't tell our mothers about it, but a lot of Saturday and

Sunday afternoons we'd stroll over to the main airport shed and sit on a bench. We got to know
most of the weekend pilots, and if one would head
alone for his plane, we'd ask if we could take a ride
with him. It wasn't long before we had clocked
thirty-seven flights in Cessnas, Piper Cubs, a dou-
ble-winged open-cockpit Waco, Aerocoups, Tay-
lorcrafts, and Beechcrafts. We never thought
about crashing, which we should have because
some of the pilots took us through stunts and let
us take the controls during level flying. We loved
the stunts—loops, stalls, spins, and wingovers—
even if they all made us feel our stomachs were
going to come up out of our throats. It was a lot of
fun. One time, we flew ten feet above the ocean
buzzing fishing boats off Sandy Hook, but the
Civil Air Patrol gave the pilot a fifty-dollar sum-
mons and a reprimand.

And, thanks to Nonno Frankie, I began to find
life much more bearable in Travis. Of course, Jennifer was my best friend, but I got to know some
of the other kids better and do things with them,
too. I became friends with Richard Cahill, Cry
Baby Rooster Head, Jeanette up the street, and
several other, normal teenagers. And even though
I collaborated mostly with Jennifer on a lot of sci-

ence and history projects, the most attention I
ever got was from something I did with Richard
Cahill. We decided to team up to write a takeoff
on a strict math teacher by the name of Mr. Stern.
We called our piece "A Geometric Nightmare,"
and it got published in our school newspaper, *The
Crow's Nest*. When it came out, a lot of kids came
up to Richard and me and said they really liked it
and thought it took a lot of guts for us to write.
Nonno Frankie went Ho! Ho! Ho! for twenty
minutes when I let him read it. To tell you the
truth, I had more friends than I'd ever had in my
life and I began to feel good about myself. I also
began to learn some of the more colorful sides to
the town, such as:

1) Travis had a volunteer fire company.
2) It had an annual Fourth of July parade at
which everyone got free ice cream and soda.
3) Christenings, showers, weddings, and funeral
receptions were held at St. Anthony of Padua
R.C. Church's parish hall.
4) A man by the name of John Steckelman had
horse teams used to haul loads of harvested
salt hay.
5) Travis first was named Travisville after

Captain Jacob Travis, a large property holder from pre–Civil War days. After that it was called Linoleumville. After that, the citizens were able to vote whether they wanted the town called Travis, Melvin, or Blue Heaven-by-the-Sea. Of course, Travis won out.

6) There were fascinating greenhouses at Mohlenoff's Florist and Farm.

7) There were a few Slavic as well as Polish residents.

8) A few grisly bodies were once found in an old quarry, which also had great frogs and gigantic snapping turtles.

9) Travis was a favorite place for torching junk cars.

10) Occasionally, sulfur dioxide fumes blew from Carteret, New Jersey, factories to engulf the streets.

11) Travis had the best view of the biggest garbage dump in the world, one receiving over ten thousand tons of garbage each day.

In other words, I was just beginning to feel like I had a father in Nonno Frankie, and a hometown for the first time in my life. I was breathing and feeling and caring about things, and trusting about being

Mom with Queenie, who she hoped was going to make her rich by giving birth to lots of dogs who looked like Lassie.

Me at a dude ranch my aunt Tillie took me to once.

NAME *Paul Zindel*

In the development of these traits, the home shares responsibility with the school.

TRAINING IN PERSONALITY	Oct. 31 / Mar. 15	Dec. 15 / May 15	Jan. 31 / Jun. 30
GOOD PERSONAL HABITS These include:			
Posture			
Sitting correctly	S	S	
Standing correctly	S	S	
Walking correctly	S	S	
Cleanliness			
Keeping hands, nails, face and teeth clean	S	S	
Keeping hands and materials away from mouth	S	S	
Using a handkerchief	S	S	
Covering mouth when coughing	S	S	
Keeping clothing clean	S	S	
Ability to dress alone	S	S	
GOOD SOCIAL HABITS These include:			
Working and playing well with others	S	S	
Responding to signals promptly	S	S	
Respecting the rights of others	S	S	

Scholarship	Oct. 31 / Mar. 15	Dec. 15 / May 15	Jan. 31 / Jun. 30
GOOD WORK HABITS These include:			
Working alone	S	S	
Doing purposeful work	S	S	
Finishing work	S	S	
EVIDENCES OF GROWTH IN:			
Ability to express himself	S	S	
Learning to read	S	S	
Speaking clearly	S	S	

S—Satisfactory

U—Unsatisfactory

I—Improvement shown

My first grade report card. It speaks for itself.

Me on the wing of a Basic Trainer 6. This plane really shook our house every time it took off.

Me sitting in a Cessna near my backyard in Travis.

Me and some kid from Travis. I could hardly ever have my photo taken without fooling around.

Miss Ella Haines, one of my teachers, on the left. I don't remember the name of the other teacher. Miss Haines was dynamic and kept us constantly surprised.

Lots of dogs who grew up to look like Lassie, but nobody wanted to buy any.

Mom in a cut-out photo from another one of her get-rich-quick schemes. She tried hand coloring photographs, but then Technicolor was invented.

Graduation from the eighth grade.

Richard Cahill and me. He and I collaborated to write a short story called "A Geometric Nightmare," for the school newspaper, in which we got even with a strict teacher. I think I look a little like a sniveling idiot here.

The Pigman's daughter and her identical twins.

The Vivona twins in a rare moment when they weren't jumping off fences or leaping out of high trees.

alive. But it didn't take long after that for the horrible things to begin to happen.

The first terrible thing was a mistake I made. I did a science project on trees, and my biology teacher was so impressed with it, she made me present it in front of the class. I showed pictures of oaks, conifers, and maples. I had samples of leaves and I discussed pollination by insects and how maple syrup was made. I had a cyclorama about photosynthesis, and a photo of a sequoia tree so big you could drive your car through a tunnel in its trunk. Naturally, I included everything Nonno Frankie had taught me, including how we had almost killed our beloved apple tree by taking the bark from half a circle around it. I explained all about the cambium layer of the tree, how vital it was, and that the life juices of all trees flow up and down through this thin living layer just beneath the bark. I noticed Moose, Conehead, and the Bronskis were fascinated with this section of my presentation, and I should have known why, but I didn't. I simply was glad to have gotten an A+.

The seed of the next disaster happened in the place where I had always been afraid something terrible would happen. Mom had begun to work nights as a practical nurse, and she had to take the eight-twenty-P.M. bus out of Travis. I remember it was a Thursday night, and I had a lot of home-work so I didn't get around to giving the dogs their evening chow until after it had long been dark. I started downstairs. The front hallway was as ghastly and chilling as ever, and I walked through the ghoulish drafts toward the side room. This time, when I got to the end of the crypt wall, I saw Nicky and Joey in the dark storeroom with their eyes glued to the lighted crack of the bath-room door.

"What're you doing?" I asked. They motioned me to shut up and to peek through the crack with them. My instinct was to ignore them and get on with feeding the dogs, but curiosity got the better of me. I tiptoed up to the crack to see what they were spying on. I knew what I was doing wasn't ethically perfect, and I felt very uncomfortable about the whole lineup of us at the "hatchet" crack. I also didn't like Connie's bedroom door open and the sight of her eight little-faced, overdressed Kewpie dolls with beady eyes staring at me from their lineup on the bed. When I *did* look through the crack, I was surprised to see it was only Connie talking to my sister, Betty, though I wondered why they had to shut themselves up in the bathroom to chat. It wasn't exactly a chat. It was more of a whisper session. Connie was telling Betty top-priority secrets. From the few words I overheard, it sounded like Connie was innocently answering a few questions about love and sex and giving Betty the kind of advice about the feelings, garments, and mechanics of passion that was a job my mother should have done years before. Of course, Mom hated love and sex so much, she never mentioned it to anybody, so I was glad Betty had someone to talk to about her being a growing, healthy young girl. I didn't listen at the door for more than ten minutes, but the twins were really glued to it. I motioned them to go back to their own bedroom, but they refused, so I left and went about my business, feeding the dogs. Nicky and Joey were still peering through the crack when I came out of the side room and went back upstairs to sleep.

The major catastrophe didn't rear its head for several days. One weekday night, Connie, Mom, me and the twins were having a dinner of leftovers from Nonno Frankie and Nonna Mamie's weekend visit. This night, it was leftover fried eggplant, an antipasto heavy on the Genoa salami, and all the garbanzo beans and baked manicotti anyone could gobble.

For some reason, Betty was late coming down for dinner, so we started without her. We were slurping and chomping away when Mom wondered aloud, "What's taking Betty so long?"

"Maybe she's having trouble putting on her *girdle*," Nicky said. He and Joey went into a spasm of giggling.

"Or maybe she's putting on red lipstick!" Joey blurted. The twins laughed so hard, they choked on their mouthfuls of manicotti.

My mother's ears went up like a Great Dane's. Her eyes zipped, radar discs focusing tightly on Joey and Nicky. Connie looked nervous, and I knew why.

"Why do you think my daughter would be putting on a girdle and red lipstick?" Mom asked the twins.

"So boys will want to kiss and neck with her!" Nicky and Joey howled.

"Who told you that?"

"We heard it."

"Where did you hear it?"

Connie sat frozen, her face red, as her kids told Mom all about their mother's nocturnal lecture to Betty in the bathroom.

"Is what they're telling me true?" Mom asked

Connie point-blank.

"Betty needed to . . . know . . . some things . . ." Connie stuttered.

"WHO THE HELL ARE YOU TO TELL MY DAUGHTER ANYTHING!" my mother screamed at Connie at the top of her lungs. Nicky and Joey stopped giggling fast and ran out of the room.

"Mom, it's O.K. . . . ." I started.

"Get out of here," she ordered.

I left the room, but I couldn't help hearing her shrieking.

"She needed to know things about love. She had questions . . ." Connie said gently.

"YOU FILLED HER HEAD WITH DIRT!"

"No, I didn't," Connie protested.

"When *my* daughter needs to know anything, I'll tell her, not you!"

"She's old enough," Connie said. "Can't you see, she's old enough and you don't talk to her about love."

"And what do you know about love?" Mom screamed. "You put on a red dress, paint your face, and throw yourself at a butcher! Don't you know what you look like when you go out? You look cheap! Cheap! You look like a clown! A dirty,

filthy clown who rolls around in the backseat of
Chops Tarinski's car! You keep your rotten, lousy
mouth shut around my daughter! You keep away
from her! You don't even talk to her, you tramp!
You low-life, filthy tramp!"

Mom stormed out of the kitchen, right past me.
I tried to tell her Connie hadn't done anything
bad, but she brushed me aside. She made for
the stairs, shouting for Betty. As she went up, I
was fast behind her. Betty came out of her room.
She *was* wearing just a little lipstick and maybe
some eyebrow pencil. Mom just shoved her back
inside, slammed the door, and screamed a lot
more. I didn't hear Betty make a sound. Mom did
all the bellowing. In five minutes Mom came
charging out.

"I'M GOING TO KILL MYSELF!" she
screamed. "YOU THINK I'M KIDDING, BUT
THIS TIME I'M GOING TO DO IT! THIS
TIME, I'M REALLY GOING TO DO IT, YOU
UNGRATEFUL STONES!" She continued shout-
ing as she ran down the stairs. "THAT'S WHAT
YOU ARE!" she threw back at Betty and me at the
top of the stairs. "TWO STONES AROUND MY
NECK! I COULD'VE MARRIED AGAIN, BUT
NO MAN WANTS A WOMAN WITH TWO

LOUSY STONES AROUND HER NECK! NO MAN!"

She exploded out into the night and was gone.

The house went silent.

No one left in the house felt like saying anything.

When I woke in the morning, Mom still hadn't come home. All I could think to do was get dressed and go out and hang out in the apple tree. A gray, wet fog still stretched from the Arthur Kill across the airport. Each step I took toward the tree felt like it was on quicksand. I refused to think of what happened the night before or what any of it would mean. As I neared the apple tree, somewhere in my heart I knew I would be losing whole pieces of myself. Mom wouldn't kill herself, I was certain, but nothing could ever be the same.

Nothing.

Then I saw the cutting marks.

The green living layer of the apple tree had been completely chopped. Someone had taken an ax and encircled the trunk with a deep, gaping wound. The wound cried out to me, the sad lips of a death mask.

I knew in that moment that Moose had slain the apple tree.

CHAPTER FOURTEEN

The Pigman's Mind-Boggling Secret!

Mom came back that afternoon. She said nothing, but Betty and I knew it was the end of our world in Travis. The final events took a couple of months, but they occurred with the inevitability of a Greek tragedy. The final shocking headlines I remember from the newspapers at that time were:

1) Swordfish Spears Teenager!
2) Cleopatra Married Her Brother!
3) Monk Steals Gallbladder Operation!

I tried to keep my mind busy reading while all the problems in our house were spelling out the split between the Zindel and Vivona families. I read one book filled with unique information, like how all the faces on U.S. coins look to the left except for the face on the penny. The book also said if I added up all the letters in the names of the cards in a deck—ace, two, three, etc.—that the total would come to 52, the same number as cards in a deck. I guess I did everything possible *not* to face up to what was happening. Most of all, I was afraid I was never going to see Nonno Frankie ever again. Connie didn't let Nonno Frankie and Nonna Mamie come to the house while there was such tension between her and Mom. She also, as kindly as possible, told my mother what I guess Mom had feared all along: She was set to marry Chops. Connie Vivona was going to become Mrs. Chops Tarinski, and the twins would have a new father. Naturally, Connie wanted her money out of her half of the house for her dowry, which meant the house would have to be sold. Mother agreed, because she didn't have enough money to buy Connie out, and because the collies still weren't selling. In fact, Mom ended up having to give all but one of the dogs away. The one puppy she sold was to the Palace Theater in Port Richmond, which ran a "Lassie Contest" in which kids were allowed to write an essay on why they would love to own a dog like Lassie in fifty words or less. A deaf teenager from Palmer Avenue won the puppy, which was a really nice touch, though I personally think the contest was benevolently fixed.

A gruff, fat real estate agent by the name of Mr. Brown got the listing for our house in July and by August it was sold. Connie and Mom didn't make more than a couple of hundred dollars each out of it, but it was better than nothing. We all had to be out by the first of September.

The final week, Jennifer cried every day. We couldn't bear to go near the apple tree anymore, so we spent many hours sitting on our favorite broken tombstone on Cemetery Hill. If I didn't have to tell the truth now, I'd just write that Jennifer and I managed to understand why we had to say good-bye, and that her fears about becoming a zombie never came true. I wish I could say she grew up, married a prince, and escaped Travis to live happily ever after in a chic condo in Malibu. But she didn't. She ended up marrying a Travis alcoholic bricklayer, and she lived for many years in the same house she grew up in, until her husband made her burn it down so they could collect the insurance money. Unfortunately, that's the way a lot of real life is. Real life doesn't always end the way you want it to. Truth *is* stranger than fiction. I think it's also often a lot more cruel. In fiction, I could make believe the morning of my final day in Travis, when Jennifer and I took our last walk, that we held hands and thought the future was going to be carefree and rosy. I wish I could write that our friendship was so intense that we wrote letters to each other for years, that we had romantic re-unions at Coney Island, Liverpool, and Madagascar, and that distance couldn't keep us apart. The only true part would be that we did hold hands on that last walk. But we said very little. We walked in the fields among the skunk cabbages and saw a muskrat run for cover. We walked by the now-dry ditch that for a short time had been our private pike pond. The apple tree stood like a night giant, black and leafless and dead. There were reminders everywhere of things that hurt. The water-head baby. The remnants of the terrarium. The pain of saying good-bye to Jennifer was so great, my mind refuses to remember it or invent it. Any teenager who's ever had to leave a best friend behind knows there are no words for it.

But I did get to see my pigman one more time.

Nonno Frankie and Nonna Mamie come down with their truck-driver colleague from NBC and the Sabatini Brothers to help Connie and the twins move.

Mom and Betty were finishing packing our junk into our old, patched-up car. I badly needed to talk to Nonno Frankie alone. I watched and waited for my chance. Finally, he was by himself in the toolshed taking apart his winepress and packing gallon bottles of his blood-red wine. All Mother had screamed for days at Betty and me was "DON'T TALK TO THEM! DON'T TALK TO ANY OF THEM!" But I didn't care if she caught me and tried to beat me with a barber strap. I went into the shed.

Nonno Frankie looked like he was expecting me. He closed the door, shutting out all the racket of the moving.

We sat on empty barrels. He wore the same oversized plaid shirt and brown baggy pants as when I first met him. He had the same excitement and energy in his eyes. It was as though everything was falling down around me except him.

He smiled at me. Not a Ho! Ho! Ho! smile. It

was a warm, gentle smile. There, amid cobwebbed windows and shafts of sunlight, he appeared to be a magical being to whom I could tell anything. Particles of dust floated in the sunbeams and moved with his every breath.

"Being different isn't enough," I said.

Nonno Frankie nodded. "No. 'Io sono differente' is not enough."

"I need to know more?"

"Yes."

"How?"

"You must climb Mount Vesuvio."

"I can't go to Italy."

"You can go in your *mind*," Nonno Frankie said. "You can go everywhere in your mind. Close your eyes and I will take you to the volcano."

I closed my eyes.

"What do you see?"

"Nothing."

"You must *imagine*."

"Imagine what?" I asked, keeping my eyes closed.

"Imagine you open this toolshed door and see a path heading up a mountain. The mountain is covered with smoke pouring down from the crater's brim. Can you see?"

"Yes."

"Now, breathe deeply and don't be afraid. Walk up the mountain path. Soon you are higher on the mountain and see a temple."

"A temple?"

"Yes," Nonno Frankie said. "It is made of white marble with hundreds of delicate cupids and baby angels carved on its arches. You walk inside and see an open coffin with a dead body lying in it. Do you see it?"

"Yes," I admitted. I was able to see anything in my mind Nonno Frankie wanted me to see. I felt frightened, but kept my eyes closed.

"You walk to the coffin and look inside. You see the face of the corpse. It is *you*."

"Me?"

"Yes. You. But different. It is you shining. It is you pure and glowing like young eggplants, and string beans, and budding sprouts. It is you before insects and poisons and witches and thirst have hurt you. Now, if you look closely, you will see the dead boy is breathing."

"Breathing?"

"Yes. The boy in the coffin is breathing, and he sits up. See him in your mind get out of the coffin. He stands before you, this *ragazzo*, this boy. Do you see him? This boy who is pure. This boy who was you. Do you see this radiant *ragazzo?*"

"Yes."

"He will tell you something."

"What?"

"I don't know," Nonno Frankie said. "Just listen to him. Look at him in your mind and let him speak to you, and you will know *more* than that you are different. This shining secret boy will let you know the answer to your question."

"What question?"

"The question you came to this toolshed to ask."

"He's not saying anything," I said. I was keeping my eyes shut as tight as I could, but the glowing ghost of myself said nothing.

"Then look in his hands. Sometimes your *ragazzo* will not talk. Sometimes he will give you a present. Look in his hands. He won't fail you. He is a perfect boy. He is a wise *ragazzo.* He will have any answer you will ever need in life. Whenever you're being attacked by witches or bullies, or starving, or confused, this boy will help you. Just ask your question."

"I'm frightened."

"*Ask.*"

"I have only feelings. I don't know the words."

"*Try!*"

"I want to know what's going to happen to me," I blurted. "What am I going to be?"

I was about to give up when I noticed something in the boy's hands. I couldn't see what it was. At first it was small, but it became golden and large and heavy. In my mind the boy gave me this piece of gold and then lay back down in his beautiful coffin. I told Nonno Frankie everything I was seeing. I told him I thought the boy had given me a large gold pipe or log. Nonno Frankie told me to keep my eyes closed, to take the gift and walk out of the temple, past the carved cupids and angels. I did. I carried the object through the vapors and down the volcano. Then I saw clearly what the magical boy had given me. A pen! A gigantic, golden *pen* five feet long and a foot thick.

I opened my eyes and told Nonno Frankie about the pen.

"There." Nonno Frankie smiled. "Your perfect *ragazzo* has told you what you are going to be."

"What?"

"You will be a *writer*."

"A *writer!*" I said, surprised. "I don't think so. I think I'm going to be maybe a chemist or a math teacher or . . ."

"No. This boy on Mount Vesuvio knows everything about you. He knows about your spook shows and your stuffed gloves with cold cream on them. He knows about your 'Geometric Nightmare' and your flesh-eating llamas. Your cycloramas and your fish ponds. He knows more than you know, which is why you must go to this *ragazzo* whenever you are in trouble. You must close your eyes and climb the volcano whenever you need him. That is the secret of life," Nonno Frankie said.

My mother went screaming through the backyard. "PAUL! WHERE ARE YOU! WE'RE LEAVING, PAUL! WE'RE LEAVING! PAUL, WHERE ARE YOU?"

Nonno Frankie and I stood up. We shook hands. I felt a chill. I opened the door and left him and a piece of my heart by the winepress. I carried a few last suitcases to the car. Mom was still yelling orders. Betty squished shopping bags and loose items into every empty cranny in the trunk and between the car seats. Soon the three of us were driving away from the tiny yellow porch, the untrimmed hedges and rickety fence. Jennifer could only wave good-bye from her porch. We drove past Mrs. Lillah, fanning herself. At the end of Glen Street Mom turned left and drove up Victory Boulevard past Cemetery Hill. Her hair flapped in the breeze from the open car windows. Betty sat silent on a suitcase.

"Our new apartment's really going to work out," Mom said, "without all those crazy, noisy Vivonas running about downstairs. I won't have to drag you kids around all over the place."

"Great," Betty and I mumbled.

"*Casey would waltz with the strawberry blonde,*" Mom started to sing, "*and the band played on. He'd glide 'cross the floor with the girl he adored, and the band played on. . . .*"